George C. Moore

Bigotry Demolished

The Close Communion Baptists Refuted, Examples Exemplified and Christian Union

Vindicated

George C. Moore

Bigotry Demolished
The Close Communion Baptists Refuted, Examples Exemplified and Christian Union Vindicated

ISBN/EAN: 9783337260613

Printed in Europe, USA, Canada, Australia, Japan

Cover: Foto ©Lupo / pixelio.de

More available books at **www.hansebooks.com**

BIGOTRY DEMOLISHED;

THE

CLOSE COMMUNION BAPTISTS REFUTED,

EXAMPLES EXEMPLIFIED

AND

CHRISTIAN UNION ESTABLISHED,

BY

REV. GEORGE C. MOOR

OF MOOREFIELD, ONTARIO, CANADA

Author of "The Life of Alexander Ca___"

Toronto:
HUNTER, ROSE & COMPANY.

LONDON: ELLITT STOCK, 62 PATERNOSTER ROW.

MDCCCLXXX.

Dedication.

TO THE MEMORY OF

THE LATE

Rev. Alexander Carson, LL.D.,

OF TUBBERMORE, IN THE PROVINCE OF ULSTER,

Of whom the Rev. Spencer Murch, of England, has recently written :—

"All Dr. Alexander Carson wrote deserves preservation. His singular worth of character; his kindly, genial disposition; his Catholic heart; his pungent pen; his reverence for God's word and truth, and his universal scholarship, *place him first amongst the sons of men.*"

THIS WORK IS FONDLY INSCRIBED,

BY HIS PUPIL AND BIOGRAPHER,

THE AUTHOR.

" I do as is my duty
Honour the shadow of your shoe-tie."—HUDIBRAS.

---

* See Appendix "B."

PREFACE.

A REASON WHY THE AUTHOR HAS WRITTEN THIS BOOK.

THE late Rev. Dr. Wills, an eminent divine and voluminous writer, formerly of New York City, gave the world reason to expect it, by the following paragraph in his work on "Christian Ordinances," published in A.D. 1852. He says:—

"Next, among many others that we think of, is the GREAT ALEXANDER CARSON, the man that was admitted by all master-minds to be in advance of his age; he, who saw so far into the truthfulness of unrestricted communion, as to declare it a *self-evident* principle, and saw about as much authority in the Scriptures for restricted communion among the Baptist denomination, as the Papists did for the doctrine of *Transubstantiation;* and it may be judged (for it is in print) from the way in which he handled that fallacy, that he would have strangled restricted communion, had he come out on it fully, as he would a lizard from a bog, upon which he might set his foot. Had his life been spared, he purposed giving to the world his views of that system, which he utterly denounced as without authority in the Word of God. But there are those* who possess his views upon the subject, given from his own lips; they tell us that possibly they shall some day give them forth in a printed form, and this is no more than the religious community will expect from them. Their testimony is, that had the Doctor written his own sentiments, the Baptist denomination must have stood amazed at the absurdity of the position they had all along been striving to defend.

"The master-mind of Dr. Carson, which would never suffer him to mince matters, led him to avow that restricted communion was contrary to all Scripture principle."

---

* Referring to the author of this work.

It has been said that "fraud deals in generalities." But whether I am chargeable, or not, with being either too particular, or general, I entreat all my Christian readers to peruse, carefully and prayerfully, both *the first and the eighth chapters of this book*. The particulars contained therein apply to all the people of God, of all sects and denominations; but *especially and emphatically to the Close Communion Baptists*. I have taken a long time to write a short book. It has been under contemplation for thirty years. I fully concur in the sentiments expressed by an ancient Roman, who said that, "Our ancestors might be contented with the immoderate and tedious length of speeches which was in vogue in those ages. As in truth, to be able to harangue for a whole day together was, in itself, looked upon at that illiterate period as a talent worthy of the highest admiration. The immeasurable introduction, the circumstantial argument, drawn out in dull variety of logical deductions, together with a thousand other impertinences of the same tasteless stamp, were then held in supreme honour. To confess the plain truth, the effect which many of the ancients have upon me, is to dispose me either to laugh, or sleep."

Were it not for my desire to favour both my publishers and my readers, I could very easily have caused my theme to fill a large folio. And as the doctrine propounded is both original and important, many may think that it needed more amplification. But though much condensed, I trust my arguments and illustrations are not obscure. I have written, not for the thoughtless multitude, but for the thinking few. From them, therefore, I crave, if necessary, a second, or even a third reading. I have traversed a hitherto unexplored region; my pathway has been heretofore untrodden. May I not, therefore, claim forbearance? I presume that the Christian world has hitherto been devoid of a scientific work on the doctrine of "*Divine Examples.*" And this fact is as unaccountable as it is lamentable. For had it been otherwise, the Kingdom of the Lord Jesus Christ might long since have been united. Not that the writer is at all sanguine as regards a successful issue, because of his feeble endeavours. The difficulties which beset a divided Christendom are too complicated and appalling to expect immediate success. My efforts and desires, however, are both heavenly and harmonizing. My wish is to have all externally united who profess to love Christ, and who believe all the fundamental doctrines of the Gospel. My efforts to convince the restricted, or Close Communion Baptists, that they are wrong in constituting Baptism the initiatory rite, or the door of admission into the Church of Christ, will apply almost equally to all Pædobaptist denominations, except the Quakers. My thanks are due to that devoted minister and eminent Oriental scholar, the Rev. Spencer Murch, of England, for an original letter on this subject, written by the peerless critic, the late Rev. Doctor Alexander Carson, of Tubbermore. For, notwithstanding the fact that the doctrine which I advocate is sustained by axioms, it is to me wonderfully assuring, that it has passed with approval through the crucible of Carson's most critical mind.

I feel constrained to say in the words of a masterly Canadian writer, the Rev. Robert J. Laidlaw, of Hamilton, that "To detect and expose the falseness that may have gathered about the religion of one's day, requires more than penetration, it demands extraordinary courage. It is easy to go forward to face physical danger, fighting in a cause which the whole community approves. A man can march right onward then, knowing that the worst the enemy can do is to kill the body. But when, for the love of Christ, a man takes issue with his best friends and despises the opinions of the whole world, and tells his own conscience that it has been mistaken, asking him to believe in things that are false; when to go forward is not only to go alone, but to go making rude war upon what men call *sacred things*, tearing them down, not knowing what structure shall be reared in their stead; to go when the enemy seems to have power to kill the soul—this is what demands courage worthy of the name. "You shall find men thick as acorns in autumn who will wade neck-deep in blood and charge up to the cannon's mouth when it rains shot as snowflakes at Christmas. Such men may be had for red coats, dollars and fame. It requires only vulgar bravery for that, and men who are food for powder. But to oppose the institution which your fathers loved in centuries gone by ; to sweep off the altars, forms and usages that ministered to your mother's piety, helped her bear the bitter ills and crosses of life, and gave her winged tranquillity in the hour of death ; to sunder your ties of social sympathy, destroy the rites associated with the aspiring dream of childhood and its earliest prayer, and the sunny days of youth—to disturb these because they weave chains, invisible but despotic, which bind the heart; to hew down the hoary tree under whose shadow the nations played the game of life, and found in death the clod of the valley sweet to their weary bosom; to destroy all this because it poisons the air and stifles the breath of the world—it is a sad and a bitter thing ; it makes the heart throb, and the face that is hard as iron all over in public, weeps in private, weak woman's tears, it may be. Such trials are not for vulgar souls; they feel not the riddle of the world."

MOOREFIELD, ONTARIO, CANADA,
August 2nd, 1880.

CONTENTS.

	PAGE
PREFACE	v

CHAPTER I.
THE AGREEMENT AND THE DISAGREEMENT OF CHRISTIANS DELINEATED 17

CHAPTER II.
THE DIVISIONS AMONG CHRISTIANS EXAMINED AND EXPLAINED—THE POWER OF FACTS 30

CHAPTER III.
THE IMPORTANCE OF HAVING RIGHT PRINCIPLES OF INTERPRETATION ILLUSTRATED 41

CHAPTER IV.
THE DIFFICULTIES TO BE ENCOUNTERED 52

CHAPTER V.
FACTS AND EXAMPLES EXAMINED 62

CHAPTER VI.

FACTS WHICH ARE NOT EXAMPLES 78

CHAPTER VII.

FACTS WHICH ARE EXAMPLES 85

CHAPTER VIII.

THE EXTERNAL UNITY OF THE CHURCH EXEMPLIFIED.. 93

CHAPTER IX.

THE PRESENT AND PROSPECTIVE CONDITION OF CHRIST'S KINGDOM 104

CHAPTER X.

FACTS WHICH PRESUMPTIVELY PROVE THE UNITY OF CHRIST'S KINGDOM 114

CHAPTER XI.

CLOSE COMMUNION MISREPRESENTS THE HOLY GHOST.. 122

CHAPTER XII.

FEARLESS INTEGRITY AN ESSENTIAL QUALIFICATION IN ACCOMPLISHING ALL REFORMATIONS................ 129

APPENDICES.

APPENDIX A.
PAGE
The late Dr. Carson and his Church at Tubbermore 141

APPENDIX B.
"The Life of Rev. Alex. Carson, LL.D." 153

APPENDIX C.
Rev. Dr. Wills' Letter 164

APPENDIX D.
God's Word the only Standard of Appeal........ 169

APPENDIX E.
Sectarianism, a Human Device.................. 175

APPENDIX G.
The Relative Position of Ordinances 182

BIGOTRY DEMOLISHED.

CHAPTER I.

THE AGREEMENT AND THE DISAGREEMENT OF CHRISTIANS DELINEATED.

Agreements and differences among Christians delineated—What Juvenal says about the Jewish bigotry—God's ways and works mysterious—Revealed things alone belong to man—Secret things to God—A prying disposition sinful—The duty of investigating all religious subjects—Christ's kingdom both uniform and multiform, fully united on all essentials, yet disagreeing about almost all non-essentials—All believe in man's weakness and destitution and slavery of sin, and in Jesus Christ as the Saviour together with the doctrines of Regeneration and Sanctification by the Holy Ghost—Agreeing about all essentials and differing about non-essentials—A paradox—Dr. Alexander Carson considered this the greatest of all mysteries—Dr. Carson's letter to Rev. Spencer Murch on Christian union and against the sentiments and practice of the Close Communion Baptists.

DR. RYAN, in his "Religion of Mankind," says, "Juvenal says that the Jews were so inhuman and bigoted that they would not point out the road to a stranger nor a fountain to a thirsty person unless he had been circumcised."

How mysterious are the works and ways of God! Everything non-essential to the earthly existence and the eternal felicity of His people is shrouded in darkness. And it is easier to realize, than it is to accept joyfully, the fact disclosed by the prophet, viz., that "revealed things belong to us and to our children, but unrevealed things belong to the Lord." Doubtless man's prying curiosity is sinful, especially is it so, when prurient, or self-aggrandizing. Certainly those who discard mystery, either in creation or religion, are sinfully unwise. <u>Those who will believe nothing, because they can not comprehend everything, must suffer the dire consequences of their contumacy.</u> To trench on the limits, or to endeavour to over-leap the lines which circumscribe revelation must be reprehensible. But it can trench on no divine right, nor can it contravene any law of Heaven, to take a microscopic view of Christ's kingdom. Contemplation and penetration when thus bestowed, can not be otherwise than legitimate, and although painful, it must be profitable.

Here we behold a kingdom which is, at the same time, both uniform and multiform. It is one and yet many! It consists in perfect unity and yet in great diversity. United in the belief and adoption of all the fundamental doctrines of Christianity without a solitary exception and still holding most tenaciously precepts, principles and ordinances, which are diametrically opposed one to the other. <u>United on all essentials</u>! <u>Dis-united on almost all non-essentials</u>!

Now, in order to illustrate, it may not be amiss to promulge a few of the essential doctrines on which a perfect unanimity prevails. Therefore, I would remark first, that all Christians are agreed in their recognition of the existence of Jehovah, the Almighty God, consisting, mysteriously, of Father, Son and Holy Ghost. Here their credence is plenary and as unequivocal as it is universal. Whereas here, if anywhere, doubts to disturb and divergences to divide might be expected to arise. But there are none. For with the docility of children, all Christians recognise God their Creator, and God their Saviour; both from the works of Creation and the Bible.

Here the Church of Christ is a unit. On this mysterious, but essential revelation, nothing heterogeneous, or discordant, can disturb their repose, or destroy their unanimity. For, although the fool hath said in his heart "There is no God;" yet to all Christians the fact that there is an omniscient, omnipotent and an ever merciful God to guide, govern and protect, is to them light, joy and salvation.

Secondly, all Christians agree in believing the humiliating doctrine of human depravity, viz., that there are by nature none righteous. This is an astounding fact. For the history of men, throughout all ages and all countries proves that all men are born Pharisees. Self-righteousness is the most inherent and prominent proclivity of human nature. Destitution, whether it appertain to that which is moral, physical, or financial, men naturally disown and discard. The turpitude ascribed by the Scriptures to their vices is by many of the unconverted considered extravagant exaggeration, or as altogether utopian. It is well known that the doctrine of universal human depravity has so enraged some self-righteous sinners, that they have blasphemed the adorable name of Jehovah and have uttered the most malignant maledictions against the Bible.

And yet, it is to be presumed, that were all the saints in Christendom congregated, not one individual of the countless host would endeavour to deny the mortifying doctrine that all have sinned and come short of the glory of God. There would, on this doctrine, be no discordant utterances from that vast multitude; because it would contain, not a solitary advocate of the moral dignity of human nature. May we not well ask, therefore, what but God's grace could have, on such a doctrine, secured unanimity from those myriads, composed of all nations, tribes and languages.

Thirdly, all Christians agree in recognising the Lord Jesus Christ, "God manifest in the flesh," as their Redeemer. All acknowledge that their manumission from sin, Satan and eternal punishment, could not have been effected by such corruptible things "as silver and gold, but by the precious blood of Christ."

What a humiliating doctrine! It certainly implies the most degrading vassalage. A vassalage of the soul instead of the body; a vassalage which is co-eval with eternity instead of time. It is the slavery of guilt; instead of that which is superinduced by indigence, or tyranny. The condition of an earthly slave is certainly the lowest guiltless position which a man can occupy. But the slave, nevertheless, may be capaple of cultivating all the virtues. He may be a man of fidelity and through the grace of God he may possess the peace that passeth understanding, together with the hope which entails life everlasting.

But wretched and degrading as human slavery is, what is it when compared with the direful slavery of sin? Both sin and Satan divest man of all moral beauty. His spiritual vision is darkness: his moral rectitude is obliqueness: his volition is enthralled and his vaunted strength is but weakness. But that which is still more lamentable is, that his vassalage renders him oblivious to his doleful degradation. Hereby we discern the marvellousness of God's grace, which so disenthrals, regenerates and enlivens, that those who were once dead in trespasses and sins are brought to accept of pardon and justification through the obedience and suffering of Jesus Christ as their Substitute and Enfranchiser. And instead of being ashamed of this humiliation, it is to them the apex of honour and dignity. Instead of degradation, it is their glory. Hark! how rapturously and harmoniously they all sing :—

> "In the cross of Christ I glory,
> Towering o'er the heights of time,
> All the light of sacred story
> Gathers round its head sublime!"

I would remark, fourthly, that they are all agreed in recognising the doctrine of Regeneration and all the other doctrines and duties which are essential to salvation. And that which seems most wonderful about this unanimity is, that it is both unconscious and voluntary. Compulsion, or coercion, is non-existent. Faith in the gospel of God, as revealed by his Spirit in the Word and the love of Christ, silently and effectually consummate this glorious agreement

How marvellous! men and women of all ages, of all countries, of all tribes, of all grades of intellect and education, and of all stations in society, from the king to the beggar, unanimously and universally, unconsciously and voluntarily assenting to doctrines which are both mysterious and humiliating seems truly marvellous!

I would remark, fifthly, that the differences and divergences of Christians are pre-eminently astounding. Surely, if the unanimity which exists amongst all Christians, regarding essentials, seems marvellous, certainly their divisions, <u>because of minor matters</u>, must be immeasurably more marvellous. For although, Feltham's theory respecting our mundane system has been denominated "glorious" because he says that "the whole creation is kept together by discord, and that vicissitude maintains the world, inasmuch as, cloud and rainbow appear together," the discord which pervades Sion may yet well be termed inglorious. What an unexampled paradox? What an inexplicable mystery? Agreeing on all essentials, disagreeing about almost all non-essentials.

Is it at all surprising that this glaring anomaly, this apparently unnecessary and unsightly dislocation in the body of Christ, should appear to be an unravelable mystery in the judgment of men of the mightiest intellect? It is well known that Dr. Alexander Carson, the great metaphysician and profound critic, frequently declared "that of all mysteries the fact that God permits His people to be divided and to fight against one-another was, to his mind the greatest mystery."

No more appropriate introduction can be given to my thoughts, and no more powerful confirmation can be given to my arguments, than the following letter (hitherto unpublished) from the pen of that renowned scholar and consecrated author*:—

"TUBBERMORE, Sept. 27th, 1841.

"DEAR SIR,

"I have received your two letters, and your reply to ———, for which I return you my sincere thanks. I am highly pleased with your strictures. I hope they will be of great service in the cause of

---

* See Appendix A.

truth. I earnestly advise you to go on with the study of the Eastern languages, especially the Syriac. For this is a new field in which you will be able to labour with great advantage, detecting the errors and ignorance of those pretenders who, from this source, are endeavouring to bring darkness over light . . . . With respect to the reception of unbaptized persons into churches, I observe that you are in doubt. There is no subject on which I am more clear; and I do not find myself in the least entangled by anything which I have advanced in my answer to Mr. Ewing. The practice of the first churches, I think myself bound to follow in every instance; but it never was their practice to reject unbaptized persons. The whole mistake arises from a false view of what is an example. A fact that could not be otherwise cannot be an example. If no believer, in the times of the Apostles, was ignorant of baptism, the fact that all persons in the Church were baptized can be no example to reject unbaptized persons.

"To be an example, it would be necessary that the persons entering should be questioned on this subject. When Paul essayed to join the Church at Jerusalem, they refused him, fearing he was not a disciple. This fact is an example, warranting us to refuse every one who does not give evidence of discipleship; but we never hear of any person asked as a condition of uniting himself with a church, were you baptized?'

"We do not need an example to warrant us to receive unbaptized persons. We have precept for it. We demand either precept or example for everything; but we do not demand both for the same thing. Now, Rom. xiv. 1, and xv. 7, command us to receive every Christian; even the weakest. <u>Baptism has reference to the truth believed, into which we are baptized, and has no reference to a church</u>. Of all things, it has the least show of an obstacle to admission into a church. It is not practised in the church at all. If at any time it is performed in the place of meeting, it is no part of the ordinances of the church.

"I believe that the first churches practised salutation. I may as well argue that no person should be admitted or retained in a church who does not practise this ordinance; and the same may be said with respect to everything in the churches. But to me, it is self-evident that every believer should be admitted to unite in everything which he understands.

"It cannot be possible that the Heavenly Father will refuse the weakest child the food that is good for him, because, from his weakness, he will not take that which is disagreeable. Besides, if baptism is necessary to unite a church, and if Christ knew that a great multitude of His people would not understand this, then different sects are unavoidable. <u>Christ must have intended to have sects</u>, and can anything be more clearly evident than that the man who has fellowship with God, may have fellowship with the Lord's Church on earth. If GOD bears with his ignorance, may not *we* bear with that ignorance? I have been written to by several of my friends on this subject, but have uniformly declined to answer, that I might not be obliged to come forward on that while engaged in so many other controversies . . . .

"I hope God will direct you, and I earnestly request you not to be rash, for I have known many who have rashly gone into this opinion, who afterwards gave it up.

"Most truly yours,

"ALEX. CARSON.

"Rev. Spencer Murch,
  Stepney College, London."

CHAPTER II.

THE DIVISIONS AMONG CHRISTIANS EXAMINED AND EXPLAINED—THE POWER OF FACTS.

What Lord Thurlow says about the power of facts—Christendom has continued divided because of ignorance or culpability—Ignorance preferable to wilful disobedience—Christians guilty of ignorance instead of disobedience—Expediency the plea of many sects—It is otherwise with the Close Communion Baptists—They believe exclusiveness to be an imperative duty—Their ideas of Apostolic example are unfounded—Their scruples to be respected—Many of them sorry for the exclusiveness of their principles—Their pathway is both solitary and friendless—Christians resemble pilgrims in a wilderness and an army in an enemy's country—The signs of the times hopeful—The re-union of Methodists and Presbyterians auspicious—The iron rigidity of the Close Communion Baptists—Carson considered close communion unjust—He did not found his practice on liberality—Bigotry founded on the wisdom of men—He was grieved because baptism is made a test of communion—Christian reciprocity sustained by self-evidence—Even small errors dangerous—The practice of the Church at Tubbermore—Rev. Mr. Lorimer's letter—Members of that Church still believe and practise infant baptism.

LORD THURLOW says: "I have seen the most eloquent speakers in the House of Commons struck dumb by a fact." The sects and denominations which have continued age after age, throughout Christendom prove demonstratively that God's people have been either culpably disobedient or lamentably ignorant. Either horn of the dilemma is as sad as it is reproachful. There is, however, an extenuating difference; because ignorance, however gross, is preferable to disobedience, howsoever trivial.

In the judgment of the writer, it requires no stretch of charity to believe, that those unsightly divisions have been produced by misapprehension, instead of wilful disobedience. For it is to be presumed that all Protestant denominations, except the Close Communion Baptists, think that union, division, or isolation, are matters which, to the churches, are altogether optional.

And there are even many amongst those diversified sects, who really believe, however fantastic, or incredible it may appear to others, that a divided Christendom is preferable to a united Christendom! Their plea, as they offer no apology for sects and denominations is, that as a matter of rivalship, a divided Church will do more for the enlargement and establishment of Christ's Kingdom, than if all were of the same name and worshipped before the same shrine. And unfortunately, the argument is far more fatal in its consequences, than it is logical in its deductions. Yet it is sufficient to satisfy millions upon millions of the most conscientious Christians.

But as regards the Close Communion Baptists, it certainly is otherwise with them. Their rule of exclusiveness and isolation proceeds not from optional, or discretionary, laws. They deem their exclusiveness to be a most imperative duty. They consider themselves bound by that which they presume to be an Apostolic example to do as they are doing without even a fractional deviation.

And it is presumable that many of the large-hearted among that great denomination are often sorry that their fanciful restrictive law is so circumscribing. Nevertheless, it were most devoutly to be wished, that those conscientious people were manifestly pursuing their solitary journey Heavenward with more signs of regretfulness, because of their having been doomed to obey this chilling, friendless and lonesome law of isolation. For, truthfully, a very sequestered and a very solitary pathway must theirs be!

How sombre and sorrowful is the lot of such a brave, though mistaken people! To see a band of pilgrims separated perpetually and unnecessarily from the mighty hosts of the Lord, is a sight which is both ungainly and ghastly.

More seemly it would be, to divide a caravan when crossing an arid wilderness, or to separate an army whilst passing through an enemy's country, than to divide God's children when on their homeward journey. In truth and verity, it verges closely on incomprehensible insanity.

C

So with an army, division or isolation generally results in utter destruction. Hence the efforts of consummate generals to have their men and munitions of war well protected by van and rear guards.

But the signs of the times are hopeful. They augur well for the unity of Zion in the immediate future. The recent auspicious union, which has been effected among the hitherto disjointed portions of the Methodist and Presbyterian bodies, renders it easily perceivable, that their differences and divisions resulted not from principle, but from feeling. Therefore, so far as those and other denominations are concerned, there can be no insuperable difficulty in the way of Universal Christian Reciprocity, or perfect external unity, being consummated immediately among all saints. Those who believe, that the King of Zion has left it as an optional matter with his subjects to march Heavenwards either in small bands, companies, battalions, regiments, or as one united formidable army, may, perchance, be easily persuaded to join the great phalanx.

Unfortunately, it is otherwise with the Close

Communion Baptists. The iron rigidity of their exclusive principle is the mountain in the way. The great effort of the writer must, therefore, be expended towards the removal of that mountain. But were I polemic, I would by no means undertake so arduous a task. The legitimate laws of controversy would enable me to cast the burden of proof on my esteemed Baptist brethren.

They affirm, that an Apostolic fact is an example, which I might only lazily and good-naturedly deny. But would this be heavenly or Christ-like, as I believe those dear brethren to be conscientiously mistaken as to what constitutes an example? No! And lest our esteemed friends should consider that I charge them exclusively, with ignorance of that which constitutes an example, let it be distinctly understood that the charge of ignorance on this subject is equally as applicable to all other denominations.

Vouchers in proof of this statement can be easily produced from the writings of the most eminent Pædobaptists. Both Drs. Miller and Hally, when writing against the Baptists, having charged the latter with inconsistency in not having unleavened bread at the Lord's Supper, have shown what mistaken ideas they also hold, about that which constitutes an example.

Dr. Carson considered close communion not only illiberality but injustice.

"Liberality of sentiment," says Carson, " is not a phrase which I admit into my religious vocabulary, for though I love and acknowledge all who love the Lord Jesus, I hold myself as much under the law of God in embracing all the children of God as in forming the articles of my creed. <u>My recognition of all Christians, I ground on the authority of Jesus.</u> To set at naught the weakest of Christ's little ones I call not illiberal, but unchristian." And when writing in the name of his church, at Tubbermore, to a Church at New York, he said: "The union of all who believe in the Lord Jesus is a thing for which we are most deeply interested, and the almost total want of it among the churches of Christ, that we deem on the whole nearest to the model of the first Church, is a thing that causes to us the most unfeigned sorrow. If that brotherly intercourse and earnest care for each other that subsisted among the churches in the days of the Apostles is not now to be found among those who profess to follow their practice as far as it was approved by Jesus, the causes ought to be sought and removed. In our opinion the chief of those causes is not the difference of sentiment, great, and greatly to be deplored, as this is, but is owing to the exercise of an authority never conferred on the churches by the Lord Jesus to refuse or exclude, for difference of sentiment, any of those who give evidence that they have been bought by the blood of Christ. Ignorance of any divine institution is an evil, and must be felt as such by a church as far as it exists in any of the body. But the question is,—What is God's way of getting rid of the evil? We believe from Phil. iii. 15, and numerous other passages to which there is not room to refer in this letter, that it is by forbearance, affectionate instruction and prayer. Many, on the contrary, have thought that the most effectual way to make a disciple receive an ordinance of Jesus, is to refuse him fellowship till he has complied. Notwithstanding all we have heard in favour of this plan, we still deem it the wisdom of man. Accordingly we have found that God has made foolish this wisdom. Long has it been tried without success: and of late, in some parts of Ireland, it has been carried so far *that some individuals can scarcely find a second to unite with them in constant fellowship. It detracts then considerably from the joy with which we should have received your letter, that we find no notice taken of this subject, but on the contrary, that you seem to make Baptism a term of communion.* We all deem that a man who has been received by Jesus ought not to be rejected by us: and that if He feed His people by His ordinances, it would be criminal in us, as far as in our power, to join in a confederacy to starve the weakest of them. We think that a man who has been admitted to the fellowship of the 'general assembly and Church of the first-born' is undoubtedly worthy of a seat with us: recollecting that if it be sinful to receive any that Christ has forbidden, it is also sinful to refuse any that He has received. There is no safe side in error! That Jesus will not approve of refusing fellowship to any of His brethren, known to be such, appears to us to have the irresistible light of self-evident truth."

The church of the late Rev. Dr. Alex. Carson, at Tubbermore, in the Province of Ulster, has alvays exemplified Christian reciprocity and external unity. Having written for information on the subject to the Rev. Wm. Lorimer, who presides over a branch Church at Tubbermore, the following extract from his letter will speak for itself:—

"Tubbermore, 15th Oct., 1877.*

REV. GEORGE C. MOORE,

Dearly beloved Brother in Jesus,—Yours of the 9th instant has been received. I am glad you are writing on Communion. You may unhesitatingly state that from the early days of the church, under the Doctor, several of the first members have re-

---

* See Appendix A.

mained ever since unbaptized, being satisfied that being sprinkled in infancy was quite enough. Not only this, but some of them even got their own children sprinkled by the parish minister of the State Church. One of these families I can myself produce in proof of this. And I am sure I shall be able to discover more.

"I don't know what they practise under the present *Curson;* but with us the old principle is carried out as in the days of the dear Doctor,—that is,—that baptism is an individual ordinance for individual Christians as such, irrespective of church fellowship altogether, and would have been the same if there never had been a Church on earth."

CHAPTER III.

THE IMPORTANCE OF HAVING RIGHT PRINCIPLES OF INTERPRETATION ILLUSTRATED.

"*It is one thing to assert a fact, but it is another thing to account philosophically for such fact.*"

The importance of Principles of Interpretation—Non-essentials not to be despised—Whatever is not commanded is forbidden—Axioms applicable to theology—Man's statements need vouchers—What Dr. Johnson says of mixed languages—My axiom regarding Baptism and the Lord's Supper—Dr. Howell the mouthpiece of the Close or restricted Baptists—Baptism his badge of discipleship—Dr. Howell mistakes facts for examples—Baptism a flimsy vestment—The Close Communion Baptists are Puseyites—The very learned and most pious Bishop Hall, his opinions and inculcations—The late Rev. Dr. Samuel Wills' delineation in his work on Christian ordinances of writers on both sides of this controversy, viz., Dr. John Gill and Abraham Booth, John Bunyan and his Pilgrim's Progress, Roger Williams and the honoured Robert Hall.

I WOULD remark 1st, that many teach and act as though things, which are termed non-essential, were unworthy of any thoughtfulness. If the soul escape the abyss of woe, and be insured a place in heaven, they seem to think that they may well forego every minor consideration. How abject! How very delusive! Why, if God has been pleased to reveal some parts of His will by types, tropes, or examples, it certainly behoves His people, to endeavour to understand such tropes, types, or examples.

Secondly, to mistake that which constitutes an example, may cause us to do that which is not commanded and consequently that which is forbidden, " for whatsoever is not commanded is forbidden."

In ascertaining our duty as taught by example, Raphael's advice to Adam, "be slowly wise," might be pondered with advantage; for they are well known facts, that men, because of mistaking the figurative language, in which our Lord couched some of His precepts, have, most inhumanly, plucked out a right eye and cut off a right arm; whilst others, in their blind zeal to obey the commission—" Preach the Gospel to every creature "—have absolutely declaimed to birds, beasts and fishes. What sorrowful and ludicrous pictures!

RIGHT PRINCIPLES OF INTERPRETATION. 43

I would remark thirdly, that the interpretation of Scripture can be neither definite nor satisfactory until self-evident principles are employed. Axioms are as applicable to some theological truths as they are to those of philosophy and mathematics. The remarks, assertions and observations, of fallible men generally need vouchers. Unless religious teachers can herald their utterances and commentations by a "thus saith the Lord," or present first principles in confirmation of their deductions, neither conviction nor conversion can be expected as the sequence. Therefore the writer would make an inroad on the disputed territory by stating that which appears to be a rule of interpretation, as clear as the light of day, viz.: That to make obedience to one law, or ordinance, necessary before obeying another law or ordinance, requires the existence of a third law, or ordinance, to point out and enforce such a necessity.

By way of analogy, I would refer to that which Dr. Johnson says of mixed languages. "A mixture of two languages," writes the great lexicographer,

---

* Whately.

"will produce a third language distinct from both."

And so I say respecting the amalgamation of Baptism and the Lord's Supper. *To make obedience to one ordinance, invariably the precursor to the other, or that which entitles to the other, must necessarily produce another law distinct from both.*

But Dr. Howell, who is the advocate and mouthpiece of the Close Communion Baptists, both of America and Great Britain, absolutely metamorphoses a mere fact into such a law. "We think," he says, "our Pædobaptist brethren Christians and we treat them as such. We regulate our thoughts and actions in both cases by the laws of Christ. One of those laws requires us to judge of men by their fruits and another obliges us to admit to the communion only baptised believers. We can receive them in the way only which Christ has prescribed." And again he says, "baptism without a profession of faith is justified as readily as the administration of the Lord's Supper without baptism." How mindless do such utterances appear when emanating from a scholar!

I would remark, *fourthly*, that the laws by which

Christ's disciples are guided and governed need to be plain and explicit.

Dr. Howell and his party imagine themselves governed by a law which never existed. Possibly, in the course of this work, it will be plainly shown, that both himself and his followers have no law for excluding any of Christ's moral disciples from church fellowship; and that they have no law to justify them in recognising as Christians, any whom they pertinaciously and persistently refuse admission to the ordinances of the Lord.

Finally, I would remark, that it must be more sinful to so aggrandize an ordinance, as to cause it to usurp the power or place of Regeneration, or Justification, than it would be to change its mode of administration, or to suppress, or supersede it altogether.

Are not the agency and influence of the Holy Ghost in Regeneration and Sanctification and the imputed Righteousness of Christ in justifying of more importance to a sinner than are all the ordinances?

What can be more lamentably subversive of the

essential truths of the gospel than the following emendations ?—

"It would not be seemly," says Dr. Howell, "to receive into our family a man destitute of garments. But it is equally uncomely to introduce to the Lord's table those who are not furnished with the vestments of the former ordinance. We have no right until Christ shall call us hence, to lay aside the habiliments with which He has supplied us and which He has commanded us to wear."

What a flimsy vestment and what a poor habiliment is Baptism! What little solace such sentiments can afford in the hour of death! Alas! that Puseyism should exist at other places besides Oxford and Rome.

How refreshing it is to listen to the erudite Dr. Wardlaw, and to the great Bishop Hall. "A Christian," says Dr. Wardlaw, "before he becomes a Baptist, is a Christian, as well as afterwards. If he refuse to commune with a Pædobaptist, it is refusing to commune with his former self.

"The Apostle also shows that Jews and Gentiles

were to forbear with one another as to days, meats, &c. It requires a little diffidence of self and a little confidence in others: a portion of liberality and a portion of charity."

What a contrast there exists between the sentiments expressed by some in this nineteenth century and those of Bishop Hall early in the seventeenth, who recommends Christians to put a charitable construction on the opinions and conduct of each other, and not disregard those who varied from them in matters of opinion concerning some appendages of religion and outward forms of administration, as if they had forfeited their Christian professions and were utter aliens from the commonwealth of Israel; though, in the meantime, sound at the heart, endeavouring to walk close with God in all their ways. " Whereas the Father of all mercies allows a gracious latitude to His children in all, not forbidden paths. Beware, ye my dear brethren, lest while we follow the chase of zeal, we outrun charity; without which piety itself would be but unwelcome.

" *Whosoever he be that holds the faith which was*

once delivered to the Saints, agreeing with us in all fundamental truths, let him be received as a brother." The Rev. Dr. Wills says, " In later days we cannot lose sight of such men as Dr. John Gill and Abraham Booth. But their strong love of party led them to display their weakness. We must ever look upon all men—the best of men—the profoundest reasoners and the soundest theologians—as coming in some respects under the influence of natural dispositions. This weak point will show itself somewhere, and did we not carefully bear this in mind, the religious world would be more paradoxical to us than it is already, and surely that need not be. John Gill, the champion of doctrinal truth and restricted communion, was naturally of a dogmatical construction of mind. It suited his natural temperament to be rigid and exclusive; a great and godly man, but not less a lover of party and the leader of a sect; conscience, however, would not let him be this, did he not consider the position to be according to the will of God. But the mind, from natural constitution, might be wooed to this conclusion, and by a plausible process of reasoning, where the premises were false, though so good and great a man, he erred. No one can read what he has written without discovering the positive way in which he advances his sentiments; and there is not a child acquainted with the Scriptures but what would be able to combat his views upon the Church, Baptism, Lord's Supper, &c. He makes strong assertions, but adduces no proof in support. He often sets down his views as though he were stating what Christ had commanded, when he has no foundation whatever in the Scripture.

So with Abraham Booth. He is viewed by the advocates of restricted communion as the unanswerable defender of their faith and practice. All who have since him written upon the subject have taken his ideas, and when they have departed it has been most evidently to expose the weakness of their position. But what candid individual who reflects when reading Abraham Booth's "Apology for the Baptists," does not discover the fabric of the mind that could dictate such a production? His assertions of the undeniable truth of his positions are strong just in proportion as they are defenceless, and he starts upon premises utterly devoid of foundation in truth. He, too, puts himself forward, as is justly observed by Robert Hall, as the champion in the cause of the Baptists. As if there were unanimity of sentiment upon the one point he proposes to sustain and defend, he calls it an "Apology for the Baptists;" and yet the whole production is against Baptists who differ in their views from him. Is not such a display of the mind of Abraham Booth enough to show how inadequate he was to such a task, when we consider the bias his mind could take of the circumstances of the Baptists in the title of his book? The venerable Booth was a godly man—a star of no small magnitude, shining with the grace of his Lord in His day on earth—but his "Apology for the Baptists" is the weakness of the man.

Having noticed the above men on the side of restricted communion, we must not forget on the other side one or two liberal souls, as great and good as have already been referred to. Who can treat with indifference the production of the famous John Bunyan—as much a Baptist as a Gill or a Booth, but breathing the spirit of his Lord and Master in favour of open communion? We must do his memory honour in this noble liberality of his soul, as much as for the singular and inimitable production of his "Pilgrim's Progress," known and regarded the wide civilized world through. Roger Williams, renowned in the history of liberty, civil and religious, in both England and America, where he took a noble part in struggles worthy of his noble soul.

Then the celebrated Robt. Hall, with giant mind, possessed acquirements and unrivalled oratory, laid hold of the horns of restricted communion, and shook the monster to a complete shadow (*).

---

* See Appendix C.

CHAPTER IV.

THE DIFFICULTIES TO BE ENCOUNTERED.

Difficulties of Archbishop Whately and opinions respecting them—Truth harder to be proved than error—Livingstone on the dividing line—Whately on Analogy and Examples—Sound judgment and discrimination necessary in observing differences—Four things necessary to constitute Facts into Examples, two positive and two negative, viz., they must exhibit both *choice* and *design*, and not be the effect either of *contingency* or of *necessity*—Gen. Scott and his defeated army at Niagara—Some facts proceed from a moral necessity, others from ceremonial and others from positive laws—The Lord Jesus was thus subjected—The Apostle Peter forgot or was ignorant of these facts—The Jews were similarly circumstanced—Having unleavened bread at the first supper a Fact, but not an Example—That which would have constituted it an Example—Those who celebrated the first supper, having been circumcised, not an *Example*—Dr. Campbell's opinion of bigots and bigotry.

THE writer fully concurs in the sentiment expressed by the late Archbishop Whately, who says that "It will often happen before a popular audience a greater degree of skill is requisite for maintaining the cause of truth than falsehood. There are cases in which the arguments which lie most on the surface are to superficial reasoners the most easily set forth in a plausible form, and are those on the wrong side. It is often difficult to a writer, and still more to a speaker, to point out and exhibit in their full strength the delicate distinctions on which truth sometimes depends." And Livingstone, a noted Scotch writer, says that "Truth is separated from error by a small, thin partition, like the edge of a razor, but God's truth lies on one side, the devil's lies on the other." The erudite Dr. Whateley also delineates the difficulties which beset the doctrine of Examples. "In this kind of argument," he says, "one error which is very common, and which is to be sedulously avoided, is that of concluding the *things* in question to be *alike*, because they are analagous; to resemble each other in themselves, because there is a resemblance in the relation they bear to certain other things; which is manifestly a groundless inference. Another caution is applicable to the whole class of arguments from Examples, viz.: not to consider the resemblance or analogy to extend further (*i. e.* to more particulars) than it does." "Sound judgment and vigilant caution are nowhere more called for than in observing what differences do and what do not nullify the analogy between two cases. And the same may be said in regard to the applicability of precepts or acknowledged decisions of any kind, such as Scripture precepts, &c.; all of which, indeed, are, in their essence, of the nature of Examples, since every recorded declaration, or injunction (of admitted authority) may be regarded in connection with the person to whom and the occasion on which it was delivered as a *known* case; from which, consequently, we may reason to any other parallel case: and the question which we must be careful in deciding will be, to whom and to what it is *applicable*. For a seemingly small circumstance will often destroy the analogy so as to make a precedent or precept inapplicable."

Let it be explicitly understood that facts which constitute examples must invariably and constituently exemplify four things, viz.: 1st, they must exemplify choice; 2nd, design; and, 3rd, they must not result from necessity; 4th, nor be the effect of mere contingency.

Mansfield, in his "Life of Scott," says, that before General Scott surrendered to the British in Canada, he ascended a log and addressed his soldiers: "Let us then die, arms in hand; our country demands the sacrifice; the example will not be lost; the blood of the slain will make heroes of the living."

The fact embodied in General Scott's resolution is a thorough exemplification of that which constitutes an example. It manifested both choice and design, and was the effect neither of necessity nor of contingency.

I would, therefore, remark, 1st, That many things were mere matters of necessity—even to the Lord Jesus Christ, there existed a moral necessity. His attributes, and the great work which He came to accomplish, rendered many of His observances, acts and utterances absolute necessities. He could not have been other than the Holy, Harmless and Undefiled. And because of His covenant engagements it became necessary for Him to die (see Heb. ii. 10, 14, 17; John xi. 49). Peter, in his blind zeal, disclaimed this principle. When his Master talked of dying, he exclaimed, "Not so, Lord, be it far from Thee." Peter seemed to have forgotten that not one jot or tittle could have been left unfulfilled of all that had been predicted of Him by the prophets of Jehovah.

2nd, There existed a necessity which resulted from both positive and ceremonial laws.

This may be termed a positive and ceremonial necessity.

Such necessities pressed heavily upon the Jews, and even the gospel dispensation is not exempt, e. g.:

Baptism and the Lord's Supper, and other ordinances are binding on all Christians by positive laws. Our gracious Redeemer, as a Jew, submitted to the law of positive necessity. He was circumcised. He observed the Jewish Sabbath. He attended the feasts. He ate the Passover and He went to the synagogue.

View Him again, as the founder of the gospel kingdom, as the leader and representative of His people, with John in the Jordan; saying,—"Thus, it becometh us to fulfil all righteousness."

His Jewish converts were similarly necessitated And His disciples throughout the past ages of His dispensation have been subject to the necessity enforced by positive laws. Paul said, "Woe is me, if I preach not the gospel." And so it has continued, and will continue evermore.

Now we can plainly see, that many things done by the Lord and His primitive disciples were necessarily done. They were not, in one sense, the effects of either choice or peradventure.

3rd. There existed also a circumstantial necessity; a necessity which emanated from time and place.

It may suffice, as an exemplification of this fact, to allude to the unleavened bread, used at the institution of the Lord's Supper. The memorative ordinance was instituted at the time of unleavened bread, and before the calling of the Gentiles. Had the Lord not instituted the Supper at the time of the Passover, unleavened bread would not have been used; and had it been after the conversion of Cornelius, the circumcised might not have been his only guests. Or had the Lord Jesus instituted this ordinance at a time when leavened bread was in use, and had He caused unleavened bread to be procured for the occasion, it would have manifested both choice and design, devoid of either necessity or contingency, and would have constituted an example to be strictly and stringently copied by His people, thenceforward and forever more. Or, had He caused leavened bread to have been procured as the material for the memorative meal, it would have manifested both His wish and will, and have demonstratively proved, that unleavened bread, was ineligible to represent His once broken, though now glorified, body. The mere fact of the unleavened bread teaches us what we may do, but not at all what we must do. As concerns the bread, all is optional and nothing compulsory.

Here I would remark that—

1. All who first partook of the Lord's Supper had

been previously circumcised. *Not one uncircumcised man was present. Is this fact an example?* Is it possible to descry a particle of either choice or design in the uttermost development of this fact? I trow not. Neither could this fact have been caused by obedience to any moral law; because moral obligations continue in perpetuity.

2. The fact of their having been circumcised is accounted for by the positive law which demanded their obedience to the Jewish rite: disobedience to it was a forfeiture of all blessing, and the precursor of death—see Gen. xvii. 14. Abraham, Isaac, and Jacob were circumcised, though they never ate either the Passover or the Lord's Supper. It is very easy to perceive, that the mere fact, that all who were guests at Christ's first supper, had been previously circumcised, betokens nothing, except that of unavoidable circumstances. Had the Lord any to communicate with Him, they must have been circumcised, because there were none others.

REFLECTIONS.

How true the trite maxim,—" That which we wish we easily believe." When reviewing my remarks about the unleavened bread, two things tended greatly to astonish me. viz.,—1st. Because some of the most thoughtful, devoted and learned Pædobaptists have considered the fact of unleavened bread having been used at the first supper, to be an example.

So confident have even Doctors of Divinity felt themselves respecting the reality of this fancied example, that they have when, I suppose, half frenzied by controversy, flung, like a barbed arrow, their glaring omission of this unleavened bread example at the Restrictive Baptists. And

2nd. Because all the Close or Restrictive Baptists do not consider it an example.

Here my astonishment is heightened. How marvellous is the wand which, by a touch, can metamorphose one fact, into a living, dictatorial example; and whose mere presence can annihilate all the pretensions to exampleship of all other facts!

Truly and well has Dr. Geo. Campbell, the great critic, said "that it is to be regretted that we have so much evidence that even good and learned men allow their judgment to be warped by the sentiments and customs of the sect which they prefer. The true partisan, of whatever denomination, always inclines to correct the diction of the spirit by that of the party."

But I am inclined to say of the Close Communion Baptists, as a great writer said of a sophistical advocate, "I admire the preacher, at the same time I condemn the doctrine." There is no sort of persons whose opinions one is more inclined to wish right than those who are ingenuously in the wrong, " who have the art to add grace to error, and can dignify mistakes."

CHAPTER V.

FACTS AND EXAMPLES EXAMINED.

A true and a false idea of examples exemplified by the French woman and the editor of *The Watchman and Reflector*—Open communion no infraction of moral law nor of positive law—Baptism and Lord's Supper not at all united, the one would exist were the other abrogated—Baptism not an indispensable prerequisite—Both ordinances instructive and comforting—God has left nothing to be learned by conjecture, nor from priority of appointment—Baptism connected with the preaching of the Gospel—Philip and the Commission prove this—Not so with the Lord's Supper—Paul left Titus at Crete to teach—Why Baptism was made an immediate duty—Baptism an individual ordinance—The Supper is otherwise—Baptism can be attended to at all times and places—Not so with church ordinances—Sects have altered both the time and the mode of administering the ordinances—The Lord's Supper administered originally every Lord's day—Were monthly administrations of the Supper Scriptural, it would fortify my argument—The way in which I account for the assumed fact of Baptism having always preceded the Supper, different from all writers who have preceded me—The Baptists of America unconsciously becoming Puseyites—*An Axiom*—Presumptiveness.

"I OWE my country an example of firmness, and I will give it."*

"To say that we receive them (*i. e.*, Saints) because Christ does it, is saying that whatever Christ does is an example for our imitation, which is fallaceous, because we cannot know the reason of His conduct, nor can we know what His conduct is in reference to given characters and individuals. He may receive multitudes that we are compelled to exclude, as he received the thief on the cross."†

How transcendantly clear are the French woman's ideas when contrasted with those expressed by the American advocate of restricted communion! The one is light, the other is darkness. One is logic, the other is jargon. The learned ecclesiastic is totally eclipsed by the courtly dame.

---

* Madame Roland of France, A.D. 1795.
† *Watchman and Reflector*, April 17, 1851.

Now, notwithstanding the tedium, and at the risk of being charged with redundancy and tautology, I must, still further, investigate this subject.

And, therefore, 1st. I would ask the restrictive brethren whether, or not, all primitive Christians were baptized before they enjoyed church fellowship, because of any *moral law?* But lest any should think that I speak as though I were ignorant of another fact, viz., that all Christians are bound, morally bound, to obey every law of God, whether positive or otherwise, I hereby avouch my faith. All are bound, morally bound, to say with God's servants of old, "All that the Lord hath said we will do." But they cannot promise to do that which He has not said, or that which He has forbidden. Had God enacted a law which interdicted any Christian from associating with His people, prior to his baptism, that law, however arbitrary it might appear, every Christian would be morally constrained to obey. Nay, did the statute books of Zion but contain the merest suggestion or innuendo, inaudibly hinting that such were the Master's wish, every true follower of the Lamb, should instantly, and with ineffable delight, render due obedience.

I would enquire, 2nd. *Was the fact caused by any positive law?* My discernment can discover no such precept. Nor do the Close Communion Baptists assume that there is. The question is put, however, in order to have the discriminating faculties of my readers invigorated. For had the opposing brethren, either moral or positive law to defend their exclusiveness, they would have blazoned that fact to the world, instead of sheltering themselves behind a nugatory, fanciful example. But they may, perhaps, remind us of the fact that baptism was anterior to almost all other ordinances, and that it was based on a positive law.

Well, this proves nothing but that which we believe and teach. Its being right to be baptized, in obedience to a positive law, cannot prove it to be either right or wrong to observe the Lord's Supper either before, or after, baptism. The positive law of baptism merely speaks for itself. Each ordinance has a separate and distinct law. Children they are

E

of the same parentage, though not of the same age. Nevertheless, were the law of baptism abrogated, it could not cease to be the duty of all Christians to commemorate the dying love of Jesus. Or, had the King of Zion seen fit to revoke the memorative ordinance, it certainly could not cease to be the duty of His disciples to be baptized. But as the mole is said to be more sharp-sighted than the eagle, for half a quarter of an inch before it, so some discerning wight may yet bless us with a sight of this Utopian law.

To the writer it seems an incontrovertible fact, that the Jews, as Jews, would have been circumcised had the Passover never been instituted; and that all believers, as believers, would originally have been baptized, had the ordinance of the Lord's Supper never been instituted. Is it not sufficient to refer for confirmation, if not demonstration, to Abraham, of the Jewish dispensation, and to the Eunuch, in that of the Gospel?

Let us now enquire, why did baptism always precede the Lord's Supper in the Primitive Churches?

To account for this fact is the appropriate work of the Restrictive Baptists and of all other Protestant Churches who hold and teach that Baptism is the initiatory rite. But hitherto they have dexterously avoided it. Indeed, nothing can be more cabalistic than the ideas which they have propounded regarding it. Yet, although it is neither my duty nor necessary to my argument, I will attempt briefly to account for it. I would, therefore, remark 1st. Baptism may have been first instituted and first observed for many reasons unrevealed to us.

But if the Restrictive Baptists cannot prove that it was first instituted and first observed as an indispensable prerequisite, or as the door into the Church, it is bootless to their cause. As yet, however, this has not been done, except by unfounded assumption and gratuitous assertion.

Nothing is more luminously shown, throughout all dispensations, than the fact that when God wished to teach His people any important duty, He never abandoned them to mystic assumption, or to mazy conjecture; *e.g.*, witness the connection between faith and works. He has not left us to ascertain this fact from the order of time or the priority of appointment: that upon which our friends erect their towering superstructure. In attempting to answer the question, reference may justly be made to the relative, or emblematical, importance of baptism, whereas it emblematises the washing away of sin, &c. But impressive and expressive as it is, were it a church ordinance, its importance could not give it precedence of that ordinance, which is commemorative of our Lord's death and sufferings. We forbear, however, drawing invidious comparisons, as each ordinance is expressive, and important, and comforting.

I would remark that 2nd. The first fact that might be adduced in accounting for it, is, that baptism had been instituted, not only before the Supper, but before the Church itself. And as a prior appointment it was natural that it should continue as it began.

The next fact that may be mentioned is:—3rd The Lord Jesus connected it with the preaching of the Gospel. The commission and the preaching of

Philip prove this. The Lord's Supper and other church ordinances are not so. Baptism was to be taught and obeyed where the Lord's Supper and other appointments were not to be even mentioned. The practice of the Apostles and Evangelists luminously shows their views of the Commission. Philip showed the Eunuch the way to Calvary, and he caused him to accompany him to the baptismal pool; but it is presumptuous to assert that he taught him any more. It was not the fitting time. To lecture the Eunuch, in the desert of Gaza, about church ordinances, would have been preposterous. To tell a man all about the constitution and privileges and duties of a Christian Church, who was not destined to enjoy its privileges, or submit to its obligations, would have been " passing strange." It would have been doing the work of a lifetime in an hour. Paul left Titus at Crete, "to set in order the things which were wanting;" so that all things might be done "decently and in order." See Acts xi. 19-26.

But our close communion brethren say with an overweening confidence: "It is nowhere said in

Scripture, believe and eat the Lord's Supper, but believe and be baptized." We reiterate the assertion; we concede the fact. Certainly, it would have been absurd for Philip to have said to the Eunuch, "believe and celebrate the Lord's Supper." But let not our friends imagine that we think so, because Gaza was far away from holy ground, or gorgeous "Cathedrals."

4th. Baptism was made an immediate duty, because it could be separately and individually obeyed. It can be obeyed by a candidate in his, or her, individual capacity. The Lord's Supper and other church ordinances, cannot be so obeyed. For although the Lord's Supper cannot be observed without an association of believers, yet Philip might lawfully have baptized the Ethiopian in the wilderness, had there not been another Saint beneath the canopy of Heaven.

5th. Baptism was made an immediate duty, doubtless, because it could at all times and in all places be immediately observed.

That baptism could be submitted to at all times

and, bating possible exceptions, in all places, the Scriptures warrant us in believing. But to predicate the same of the Lord's Supper—to assert that it could have been observed at all times and in all places—would be obviously unfounded. For, although the jailor was baptized at midnight, and the Ethiopian was baptized in the wilderness, yet the Scriptures inform us that the disciples had to congregate, in order to observe the commemorative ordinance: "And upon the first day of the week when the disciples came together to break the bread." In other words, they had to come together to do that which Paul reproved the Corinthians for not having done aright: "When ye come together into one place, this is not to eat the Lord's Supper." See 1 Cor. xi. 20.

Be it observed that, in our own times and in all times since, some Churches audaciously arrogated to themselves the power of enacting laws, and of changing ordinances, a convert to Christianity could not and yet cannot possibly attend to the Lord's Supper, for the first time, for the space of from one, to three months. Were a man, or woman converted amidst the great body of Restrictive Baptists, those who profess to be, *par excellence*, scrupulous copyists of all primitive examples, such convert could not, if converted early in any month, observe the ordinance of the Supper, until after several weeks had elapsed. Alas! Alas!

But it is easy to perceive, however, that such monthly and quarterly customs, were they scriptural, would help to fortify my position, and that they would proclaim to the world, that baptism was made, a first and an immediate duty, because it could be immediately obeyed.

Now, I have reached the goal. When starting I tasked myself with the solution of the question, whether or not our Lord and His Apostles acted under the authority of moral, or of positive law, in associating exclusively with baptized persons. And if not guilty of some mental obliquity, I think I have shown, that the necessity under which they acted, was merely circumstantial.

But, suppose I had even failed in accounting satisfactorily for the disputed fact, what follows? Not the failure, or the absurdity of my arguments, or principles. It were naught, save the failure of an attempt to convince those whom I think in error, but whom, nevertheless, I esteem and love. I invite my readers to compare the way in which I have accounted for the priority of Baptism—especially with that to which it is ascribed by the Close Communion Baptists. Dr. Howell, their chief advocate has declared that unbaptized Christians ought not to be received into church fellowship because it would be receiving them without "*sufficient evidence of grace in the heart.*" The way in which I have endeavoured to account for the fact, neither unduly exalts baptism, nor in any sense, or to any degree, depreciates its importance. It is neither made absolutely essential, nor is it at all, set aside, as a nugatory rite. It is assigned its respective province in the Gospel dispensation; but that province, is not that of being the badge of discipleship, instead of love; nor that of being the door into the Church of Christ, instead of Christ Himself, nor that which washes away sin, instead of the precious blood of Christ which atones.

RETROSPECTION.

Most gladly would I have retired at this stage, to allow my readers to contemplate, calmly, the arguments which I have submitted. But there is an eye-sore, a gangrene, which so irritates my spiritual vision and gnaws my spiritual entity, that I cannot pass it by silently.

What save the temerity, engendered by denominational prosperity, or the desperation which accompanies despair, could have induced a doctor of divinity, an otherwise orthodox doctor of divinity, to have constituted baptism the insignia of "grace in the heart!" Verily, this great section of the Baptist denomination are, most unfortunately and unconsciously, becoming the veriest Puseyites!

How very different are the sentiments advocated by Dr. Howell from those of the Apostle Paul, and those upon which Abraham Booth descanted in his "Reign of Grace." How the descendants, or coreligionists, of Andrew Fuller and Joseph Ivamy, of Kinghorn, and Norton, of England, together with those of the Rev. Drs. Fuller, Williams, Cone, Wayland, Hague, and Duncan Dunbar, of America, can brook such teaching seems truly marvellous? What? Baptism the only efficient, or sufficient evidence of grace in the heart!

Shade of the Martyrs and of the Confessors and Reformers come forth as a phalanx of light to contradict and controvert this flagitious falsehood! Baptism the only efficient, the only potent, the only satisfactory evidence of grace in the heart!!

Look! look my readers, at the hosts of baptized apostates, who have infested the world, since the days of Judas Iscariot, Simon Magus and of Julian the apostate; and say, what evidence is baptism, either of conversion, or discipleship!! I will here state that which I consider an incontrovertible axiom, viz.:—

That, the existence of that which, in no sense and to no extent, qualifies a man, its non-existence can, in no sense, and to no extent, disqualify him.

PRESUMPTIVENESS.

"The aggregate of all those sects and systems is popularly known as the Church, and the Church is acknowledged to be of divine institution. Some claim that only their own sect is of divine appointment; but this claim now meets with general disfavour. The disposition on the part of any particular branch of the Church to lay claim to being the veritable Zion the Lord hath founded, arises from a misconception of what is meant by Zion, and a misunderstanding of the purposes for which the Church has been established. They imagine that by Zion is meant not a kingdom whose throne has been prepared in the heavens, and all whose appointments are adjusted with reference to the circumstances and wants of the subjects, but an artificially contrived system, having certain parts and functions arranged upon an arbitrary plan and founded for its own sake, or at best for the purpose of glorifying God, through its beauty and perfection as a system. Those who hold this view glory in their Church as a visible institution, having, as they believe, exclusive divine authority for every article in their system of church government, and for each particular feature in their forms of worship, and for every clause in their Church's creed. They contend for the Church as an outward organization. It must stand forth as a sacred structure whatever becomes of those who refuse to bow down and worship. Its appointments must move along from age to age in stately and monotonous procession even though they should crush the erring and the helpless beneath their tread." *

---

* See Appendix E.

CHAPTER VI.

FACTS WHICH ARE NOT EXAMPLES.

Contingencies have been metamorphosed into examples—Unleavened Bread—Celebrated at night and in an upper room not examples—All Primitive Christians baptized before observing the Lord's Day—The Gentiles had no Sabbath, and the Jews observed the Seventh Day Sabbath—This fact showed neither choice nor design—Primitive Christians enjoyed miraculous powers, and spoke unknown languages—Were those facts examples, Christendom would thereby be now *unchurched*—The emanation of an Italian writer—Dr. Buchanan and Bishop Hall's opinions.

BEFORE proceeding to particularize facts which constitute examples, it may be profitable to glance at a few of those primitive contingencies, which have been frequently metamorphosed into examples.

I would remark that: 1st. *Having used unleavened bread, and celebrating the first supper in an upper room and at night, are not examples.*

But as the Close Communion Baptists do not claim the authority of exampleship for any, or either of these facts, it seems bootless to enlarge. And if any person or party wishes to know why, I refuse to recognise the exampleship of all such facts, such person or party may find my reasons therefor in a previous part of this work. The writer wishes to avoid verbosity and supererogation.

2nd. All Primitive Christians had been baptized before they observed the Lord's Day.

It seems to be indubitably certain, that all Christians originally were baptized before they observed the Lord's Day.

The fact that the world was divided into Jews and Gentiles, and the conceded fact that, originally, the first duty attended to by every convert to Christianity, was baptism, proves conclusively the truth of the proposition. For,

1st. The unconverted Jew would not abandon his own Sabbath; so long as he acknowledged fealty to his ecclesiastical kith and kin. He believed neither in "JESUS OF NAZARETH" nor in His laws, nor His institutions. In his unenlightened judgment, the observance of any day which tended to supersede his hoary and time-honoured Sabbath, must have appeared to be a sacrilegious spoliation. And

2nd. The unconverted Gentile, slighted both the Jewish and the Christian Sabbaths. He cared for neither. Hence the fact, that the Gentile must have been baptized before he celebrated the Lord's Day.

Now, I may ask with calmness and confidence, do these facts manifest either choice or design. Would it have contravened any law of Heaven, to have allowed such converts to have celebrated the day which proclaims Christ's resurrection, had any of them remained unbaptized, because of any adventitious circumstances? For if the Lord's Supper be an appointment of the Lord, so also is the Lord's Day an appointment of the Lord. If the one appointment celebrates His death, the other appointment, for ever more celebrates His resurrection. How anomalous, how marvellously inconsistent, is the conduct of our restrictive brethren! They cordially, yea cheerfully, unite with all Christians, whether baptized or unbaptized, in celebrating the Lord's Day. Whereas, they look awry, upon all without their circumscribed circle and deny their right to celebrate the Lord's Supper. Why do they not bewail the degeneracy, decry or impugn the motives and condemn the sacrilegious temerity of all pædobaptists, because they celebrate the Lord's Day? Fortunately, their sanity over-shadows and countervails their inconsistency.

4th. The *Primitive Christians were endowed with miraculous power, and with speaking unknown tongues.*

Are these facts examples? It seems propitious to the cause which I advocate, that those facts existed. For since the churches became denuded of these superhuman powers, none but maniacs could presume to claim for them the authority of examples. Indeed, no axiom in Euclid can be more incontrovertible than that,—"*that which to us is an impossibility cannot be an example.*"

Were it believed universally that these facts constitute examples, what desolation and mourning it should necessarily engender throughout Christendom! The mind stands aghast at the spectacle! What a spiritual deluge would such examples hurl all over the extensive kingdom of Emmanuel! By their arrant disobedience and constitutional deficiencies, all churches would inevitably become unchurched. Were miraculous power, one of the essential and component qualifications of a Church of Christ, then the spiritual poverty, the absolute mendicancy, of all professors of Christianity, in this age, might well make them, either innocent dupes, or arrant impostors.

An Italian writer, when descanting on the Acts of the Apostles, says:

"The difficulty to the Jews of receiving the Gentiles was a great one. To do so was to give up all their privileges: all that remained of the ancient glory of Israel. Peter, therefore, on his return to

Jerusalem, is reproached; he had eaten with the Gentiles. Peter narrates all that had happened, and how God had given them the gift just as to believing Jews; how then could he hinder God? The Spirit had sent him to the Gentiles—the Spirit had been given to them. It was the accomplishment of the words of John the Baptist, and other brethren were witnesses to the gift of the Holy Ghost. The Jews could no longer resist the clear evidence of the will of God. Grace overcoming in their hearts, they exclaim—'Then hath God also to the Gentiles granted repentance unto life.'"

Dr. Buchanan, another great man discourses thus:

"What kept the old Roman soldiers together when at war, was the common homage paid by them to the Imperial Standard, which floated over the Prætor's tent. So again, when the ancient Scotch warred with the English, it was not the pennons of the various Feudal chiefs, but the broad banner of Scotland, which kept them together against so formidable a foe."

" The celebrated Bishop Hall, said above two hundred years ago, that he considered that if those who consented to the chief specialties should fall out about immaterial differences, they would be like to quarrelous brethren, who having agreed upon the main division of their inheritance, fell out about some heaps of rubbish."

CHAPTER VII.

FACTS WHICH ARE EXAMPLES.

Close or Restricted Communion causes sects and divides Christ's body—Choice and design essential in facts which constitute examples—The Lord's Day—The Jewish, or Seventh Day, Baptists—The cause of their practice—2nd, The Lord's Supper—Strange that those who observe the Lord's Day because of the law of example neglect doing the same with the Lord's Supper—Evidently caused by misapprehending the phrase " as *often* as ye do this," &c.—Why the Church at Corinth was reproved about the Supper—The Baptist Church at Abbey Street, Dublin, its forbearance—The downfall of idols at Christ's birth—The Ants, their unity and confraternity—Ants are worthy of imitation by many Christians—The ancient Romans were emulous of imitating their ancestors.

" THE principles held by the Close Communion Baptists would force Christ, had He acted on their plan, to make two sets of law for His Church, as it would make two parts of His body. They are very unkind to the lambs, they leave all to the foxes."*

Facts which constitute examples invariably manifest both choice and design, and are neither matters of contingency nor of necessity. Now for an exemplification of the principle. The first to which I will advert is, *The Lord's Day.* The accounts furnished by the Acts of the Apostles and the Epistles show clearly that the Primitive Churches observed universally the Lord's Day. And church history proves that those churches which succeeded the Apostolic, continued to do so. Herein is a perfect example. Had it pleased the King of Zion, to have perpetuated the Jewish Sabbath, he would have caused His people to have continued the observance of their Jewish rite.

There is a small section of the Baptist Church in America who in their blind zeal still observe the seventh, instead of the first, day of the week. They

---

* Alex. Carson, LL.D. Uttered A.D. 1844, but hitherto unpublished.

are generally denominated "Seventh Day Baptists." I mention them not, however, as a subject for condemnation. Because their scrupulous adherence, to a custom, which they deem scriptural, deserves as much praise, as their ignorance of that which constitutes a divine example, deserves lamentation. But as all other churches are unanimous in their adherence to the Lord's Day, the subject needs no further amplification.

2nd. The Lord's Supper.

"I believe I am no more at liberty to disregard what I find in the Word of God respecting every pin of the Tabernacle than I am at liberty to disregard what I find there respecting the salvation of my soul. Whatsoever I find in the Word of God respecting any arrangement which He has laid down for the regulation of my conduct I am bound to follow to the best of my ability." *

It were well that all Christ's disciples had heretofore practically adopted the sentiment so lucidly

---

* Speech at Glasgow on "Christian Union," by Dr. Candlish, A.D. 1845.

avowed by the learned Dr. Candlish. It seems strange that the greatest part of those who pertinaciously abide by the examples set by the Primitive Churches as regards the Lord's Day act as though they were freebooters respecting the example left them by the Apostolic Churches regarding the Lord's Supper. For if it be a fact that all primitive Christians assembled on every Lord's Day, it is unquestionably certain that whenever and wheresoever they so assembled they all ate the Lord's Supper. See Acts xx. 7 ; 1 Cor. xi.

Evidently this dereliction of duty is caused by misapprehending that which constitutes an example, and by misinterpreting the words uttered by the Lord Jesus when inculcating the purpose for which the ordinance is to be observed—"*as often as ye do this* do it in remembrance of me." The Church at Corinth was unsparingly rebuked by Christ's Apostle for having forgotten the purpose, notwithstanding their sleepless exactitude as it regarded the time. "When ye came into one place this is not to eat the Lord's Supper." The one was outward and visible, the other was inward and invisible. The recurrence of the Lord's Day, rendered the time tangible and obvious, whereas the purpose could only be comprehended by the upheavings of faith. When, oh, when! shall all the Churches of Christ resume their allegiance to their rightful King, by observing this ordinance, both as regards its *time* and its *purpose* ?

One of the most striking exhibitions of Christian reciprocity, which the writer has ever witnessed, is cultivated every Lord's Day by the Baptist Church which worships in Abbey Street, Dublin. Many of the members of this ancient Cromwellian Church, believe in the monthly celebration of the Lord's Supper, whilst others observe it weekly. All are agreed to differ, both as regards principles and practice. Here, undoubtedly, is a model Church. Here diversity of opinion exists, conjoined to infrangible unity. Let all Christians cultivate this spirit of forbearance and Christ will shortly have as united a Church as that which was founded by the Apostles.

Universal charity can accomplish that which

never has, and never can be, effected either by rigid or frigid uniformity. How true are the words of the great Carson *—" Where Christians have perfect harmony among themselves it is the harmony of ignorance."

3rd. *The Apostolic Churches admitted those who were weak in faith and those who were prejudiced into church membership.*

It has been said that when Christ was born, all the idols in the world fell. But whether this be a genuine truth, or a mythological legend, it is certain that all barriers and impediments to a full and free reception into Christ's original Church, fell flatly before a profession of faith in the Son of God. The mandate from Heaven was—" Him that is weak in the faith receive ye." "Who art thou who condemneth another man's servant? To his own master he standeth or falleth."

The story of the ants, as related by Mr. McCook may be appropriately quoted.

When speaking of the habits of Fornicarufa, he

---

* Alex. Carson, LL.D. Uttered A.D. 1844, hitherto unpublished.

says that the "ants, when descending the tree paths with abdomens swollen with honey dew (called by him Repletes) were arrested at the foot of the trees by workers from the hill seeking food. Galleries communicating with the hills opened at these points around, and in which numbers of ants were huddled engaged in drawing or bestowing rations of honey dew. Similar commissary stations were found under stones near by. The Replete reared upon her hind legs and placed her mouth to the mouth of the Pensioner, who assumed the same rampant posture. Frequently two, sometimes three, Pensioners were thus fed by one Replete. Apparently the workers engaged in building the hill and galleries had thus resorted to those feeding places to obtain ordinary food, in the same manner that Queens, males and young ants receive it, viz., by disgorgement from the abdomen of the Repletes. The latter commonly yielded the honey dew complacently, but were sometimes seized and arrested by the Pensioners with great vigour.

"A number of experiments were described, leading

to the conclusion that there *was complete amity between the ants of a large portion of the field*, embracing some 1,600 hills and countless millions of creatures. Insects from hills widely separated, always *fraternize completely when transferred*. A number of ants collected from various hills fraternized in an artificial nest, harmoniously building galleries and caring for the cocoons."

Am I not as justifiable in referring those in Christ's Kingdom who are "heady and high-minded," domineering, selfish and ungenerous, or rash and irascible, to be taught by these insects, as was Solomon in sending the sluggards to their school? For verily, they teach unity, amity, generosity and fidelity as fully as that of industry. How much superior was the fraternal spirit manifested by the infidel Romans when compared with the fratricidal spirit exhibited, age after age, by the nominally christianized Romans. One of the Scipios declared that he could never view the figures of his ancestors without finding his bosom glow with the most ardent passion of imitating their deeds.

CHAPTER VIII.

THE EXTERNAL UNITY OF THE CHURCH EXEMPLIFIED.

Excision and Unity taught by examples—Professor Curtis another mouthpiece—His distinction between Christian and Church fellowship a myth, an unfounded assumption—his cause is pitiable—He could not succeed had he written as many books as Epicurus, or Varro, or as Origin, or Didymus—The absurdities embraced by the human mind marvellous—Had the Apostolic Church bestowed Christian Fellowship upon those whom they excluded from church fellowship it would be an example.—Had there been anciently both baptized and unbaptized believers, and the baptized had been received and the unbaptized had been rejected it would be an *example*—But there existed one class only—There existed only one denomination which is an Example—Dr. Struthers' sentiments—There are many Alphonsos.—Wonder that Christ did not allow of two denominations: a *Jewish* and a *Gentile Church*—It would not have rendered Him bankrupt—The Romans had no word to express what we call "common sense"—The poverty of all languages when delineating this and some other subjects—This is the plainest and most unmistakeable example—It cannot be mistaken—Inculcated by the Lord Jesus and His Apostles—The primitive unity not caused by *necessity*—Carson's opinion of that which *qualifies* members for membership.

PROFESSOR CURTIS, of the United States, another mouthpiece of the Close Communion Baptists, has written a volume in a futile endeavour to establish a difference, or a distinction between *Christian and Church fellowship*. Seldom, indeed, has the Christian world been afflicted by such an exhibition of sophistry. Direful, or pitiable, must be the cause, which needs such advocacy. But he deserves no attention from me, as the principles propounded in this work must necessarily prove that his theory is no better than legerdemain. Had Dr. Curtis written books after this fashion, until they outnumbered those written by Epicurus, or Varro, Origen, or Didymus, they would tend only to sink the casue he advocates, more deeply, in his sophistical quagmire. His efforts are all perfectly quixotic.

Marvellous are the absurdities often embraced by the human mind! Truth, certainly, is sometimes stranger than fiction. But how any man, or body of men, can complacently fraternize with other Christians, supremely orthodox and strictly moral Christians: many of them zealous and eloquent ministers of the Gospel, and yet look to the Book of God for an example to justify them in debarring such from any ordinance in Christ's Kingdom, almost surpasses the conjectural powers of the most fertile imagination.

The system adopted by our restrictive Baptist brethren and by all other denominations who may be guilty of excluding moral and orthodox Christians, because of some minor nonconformity, is not only incongruous and incompatible with Scripture, but is truly the baseless fabric of a vision. It is buttressed upon neither theology, reason, nor common sense. Henceforth they may look in vain for an example to justify their untoward and unwarrantable practice. Manifold and marvellously great has been the charity vouchsafed to them by the

Pædobaptist world. Embraced as brethren, and yet anon repulsed and disowned as aliens. Had their practice emanated from arrogance or assumption, it would positively be unendurable. But presuming it to be the offspring of an easy credulity and fiery zeal, it becomes tolerable.

It is to be hoped and prayed for, that hereafter and unceasingly, the Holy Ghost may beget in them a spirit of consistency by which they may be constrained to admit to all ordinances and full church-fellowship, all the orthodox and moral disciples of Christ throughout Christendom, or, otherwise, to disown them always and to discard them everywhere. To say, as Dr. Curtis does, that Christian fellowship was bestowed before church fellowship in Apostolic times, is no argument. Had the Apostolic churches extended Christian fellowship to those whom they had excluded from church fellowship, it would have been an example to justify the Close Communionists in acting similarly.

2nd. *A supposed fact which would have been an example.* It may be well before closing this section to state explicitly for the behoof of the Close Communion Baptists that which would have been an example, ample and explicit enough to justify their exclusiveness, viz., That had there existed in the days of the Apostles both baptized and unbaptized believers, and had the primitive churches, invariably and everywhere, received the baptized into church fellowship and refused admission to the unbaptized, that fact would have been a veritable example; a model to be imitated by all churches for evermore. This fact would manifest both choice and design most perfectly.

But as there existed one class only, there existed no opportunity to manifest either design or choice, it was merely the enforcement of a circumstantial necessity. How simple the solution of this hitherto difficult problem! How easily this perplexing labyrinth has been disentangled! Can anything be plainer? Can anything be more conclusive?

3rd. ALL APOSTOLIC CHURCHES WERE OF ONE DENOMINATION AND WERE EXTERNALLY UNITED.

This fact is an example. Dr. Struthers has well

said,—" That those who love their system on account of its founders because they were good and great men, are guilty of that for which Paul reproved the Corinthians, 'Who is Paul and who is Apollos, &c.'"

Come hither, ye sectaries of all lands and of all Christian ages, and behold your distorted forms in the mirror of this divine example. It cannot do otherwise than blazon forth to your hazy vision your obliqueness, unfaithfulness, and culpable degeneracy. The temperaments which engender discord and division seem indigenous to human nature. For even in the days of the Apostles many were adventurous enough to display their proclivities. It is said of Alphonso the Infidel, that in his blasphemous arrogance he declared that if he had been with the Creator, when he was creating the world, he could have taught Him a lesson. Impious mortal! Facts evidently indicate that there have been many Alphonsos. How many there be, even in our own enlightened age, who, had they lived contemporaneously with the founders of Christ's

Church, would have volunteered an opinion, or who might even have hazarded an advice on this momentous subject!

The idea of having all Christians shackled within the tightening, the suffocating meshes of one denomination, would, doubtless, have appeared to their democratical souls both parsimonious and preposterous. Two denominations, at least, would be deemed essential. One to be denominated the *Jewish Church* and the other the "*Gentile*." To the writer, even, it sometimes appears mysterious that the Lord Jesus, who knew the separating propensities of his future flock, did not gratify this propensity to a limited extent. The limited indulgence of allowing merely two denominations would have been but a doit, a mere mite, when considered in connection with the overflowing effulgence of the Exchequers of Heaven. But no! not even an inch, much less an ell, of marginal latitude did He allow! The Jew and the Gentile, notwithstanding their previous feuds, hatred and recriminations, must, after their conversion from darkness to light, after having been adopted into the family of God, be henceforth called by the same name and be dwellers together as subjects of the same King, as children of the same Father, and as coheirs of eternal life and blessedness.

Scholars know that the Romans had no word in their language by which they could communicate that which is expressed by our words "good sense." And when a man comes to grapple a subject of such gigantic dimensions as that presented by my theme, he feels the poverty, yea, the beggary of all languages. It acts on the mind as an insupportable load,—an unutterable perplexity. Because, this is an example which seems to be above and beyond all other examples. For the lesson which was intended to be perpetually taught by it, was made manifest by the prayers offered up by the Lord of life and glory, before His ascension.

"Neither pray I for *these* alone but for them also which shall believe on Me through their word." "That they all may be one as Thou Father art in Me and I in Thee, that they may also be one in Us,

EXTERNAL UNITY OF THE CHURCH. 101

that the world may believe that Thou hast sent Me. And the glory which Thou gavest Me I have given them that they may be one even as We are one. I in them and Thou in Me, that they may be made perfect in one."—John, chap. 17. Who could have imagined at the time when those prayers were offered, that those for whose behoof they were presented, would afterwards continue disunited! A divided Church is a picture, which is both sad and sickening. Who can refrain from exclaiming " Lord, what is man that Thou art mindful of him, or the son of man that Thou visitedst him ?"

And the same matter of Christian reciprocity, or perfect internal or external Christian unity was expressed absolutely, and dogmatically inculcated by Christ's Apostles. So, whatever excuse, the ignorant and the obtuse may have, in having misunderstood and disobeyed the duties, inculcated by other examples, all shifts and subterfuges must fail, if alleged against it. For this example is like the 53rd chapter of Isaiah, of which a Jew once said, "that there was no difficulty in understanding the 53rd chapter of Isaiah; the great difficulty was, in not being able to misunderstand it." And so it is with this unspeakably prominent and lucid example. Its light is replete and evidential.

Moreover, the fragmentary confederacies into which Christ's people have respectively constituted themselves, may easily see that this example was not caused by "necessity," that which Milton denominates "the tyrant's plea." For had the Great Head of the Church allowed sects and various denominations to exist, it certainly would not have been the infraction of any law, moral or ceremonial, positive or circumstantial; and beyond all doubt or peradventure, it is infinitely removed from contingency or haphazard: because choice and design are legibly and indelibly stamped upon its forehead.

That late excellent minister of Christ, the Rev. James A. Haldane, has said that "a Church of Christ is a free school for all His disciples, and no man is warranted to exclude even the weakest and most ignorant." Certainly the Scriptures inculcate the law of love. And we have neither a command nor an example for loving as Christian brethren, those who are denied admission into the Church, or those who have been excluded therefrom. *It would be strange to see a man die for one with whom he would not, or could not, hold Christian fellowship. See* 1st Cor. 13th chap. And *we are commanded to lay down our lives for the brethren:* that which we are not bound to do for any persons besides. Christians individually and collectively are glaringly inconsistent in awarding sincerity to those whom they disown and repel. Dr. Alexander Carson has well said:—"that which takes a man to Heaven ought to take him into any church on earth."

Who can be astonished at the sentiment expressed by the poet?—" Man's a biped, amphibious both in nature and religion; and the least that is said about him the better!"*

---

* See Appendix F.

CHAPTER IX.

THE PRESENT AND PROSPECTIVE CONDITION OF CHRIST'S KINGDOM.

Man's mind strangely constituted—Decartes, his scepticism—Christ's Kingdom is divided—Melancthon and the wolves and the dogs—The dogs were of many colours—A divided church is a weak church—Too many city and village pastors—Dr. Symington's sentiments—Christ like the sun—His Church like an army—Dr. Cox and the Waterloo soldier—Christians might learn wisdom from worldly kingdoms—The Hippomolgians loved peace—The Indian king or chieftain hardened in idolatry by the divisions of the missionaries—Homer and the fishermen of Io.—The Church will continue to be feeble and divided until she becomes more prayerful—Homer's heroes—The cause of their success—Hector, the Trojan Hero, the Hosts of Greece pray for success—Poetry—Pope's translation, Livy and Cicero and Balbus the Stoic believed in supernatural agency—The Motto of Cyrus, "*Jupiter the Defender and Conductor*"— His motto not so assuring as that of the

Christian—Christian unity and reciprocity inculcated—Christ's Benediction deserves both consideration and anticipation.

"*Obedience is the first duty of every soldier.*" *

WHAT strangely constituted minds some men inherit! It is well known that Descartes did not believe in his own material, or bodily, existence, except as the result of a mental deduction. *Cogito ergo sum* was his only voucher, or trustworthy evidence to the existence of his corporeal frame. Poor drivelling philosopher! who will say that thou wast any wiser than a maniac? Dr. George Campbell has declared that axioms are not self-evident to all minds.

I would remark—

1st. *That Christ's kingdom is a divided kingdom.* Dr. Struthers says that "Bassarion, when exhorting the Christian princes to join against the Turks, tells a story about the dogs and the wolves which Melancthon applied to Christians in his day : 'There

---

* Sir Henry Pottinger, Gov.-Gen. of India.

was a war between the wolves and the dogs. Tidings were brought to the wolves that there was a huge army of dogs coming against them, to tear them in pieces. The wolves sent out an old cunning wolf to survey them, and to act the part of a scout. On his return he told them that there was indeed a great company of dogs coming; they were far more numerous than themselves; but they need not fear, for he perceived they were of different colours. On hearing this the wolves disregarded them.'"

It must be admitted that a divided church must necessarily be a weak church, for "divide and devour" is the motto of every enemy. Division necessarily weakens the Church numerically, financially and spiritually. Village hamlets, as well as towns and cities, have many superfluous places of worship. One minister of the Gospel might preach to all those who now employ, it may be, six or eight ministers.

I cannot well avoid adducing the thoughts of another celebrated divine. "All Christians," says Dr. Symington, "are of one family, of one flock, of one kingdom. In Heaven there is a unity of views

—they see and think alike. There is a unity of affection. See 2 John i. 2; Phil. i. 9. There is unity in the worship of the heavenly Church. Rev. iv. 10. The Church is one in liberty and holy obedience,—it should be so upon earth. Christ, like the sun in the firmament, is the great central orb. The Israelites, when marching to Canaan, went to war, marshalled as one mighty host, and led by one leader, though under their respective banners. There were four divisions, but all followed Judah as the vanguard in the march."

Here we have a vast multitude and yet perfect order. There is multitude, distinction, union and order. Every man stood by the ensign of his father's house; every tribe by its own standard; every battalion by its banner; and all were led by the ensign and captain of Judah. The late Rev. Dr. Cox, of Hackney, happened to be either working or walking in his garden, in the memorable year 1815, as a limping soldier was passing by. The Doctor asked him if he was a soldier. He replied affirmatively. Being asked where he had fought, he replied, " WATERloo.' The Doctor then asked him if it was for the company (the 61st) to which he belonged. The old soldier seemed indignant, and, drawing himself up to his full height, he replied, "I fought not for the 61st, but for the liberties of Europe."

What lessons of wisdom, consistency and peacefulness are taught the Church of Christ by men of both ancient and modern wordly kingdoms! Homer, in one of his sublime passages, represents Jupiter as taking off his eyes with satiety from the horrors of the battle-field, and, by way of relief, as turning his gaze upon a people called the "HIPPOMOLGI," who were famous for their simplicity and habits of quietude. Would that the demeanour of every individual Christian were such in the family, in the camp, and in the whole domain of Christ, that he, or she, might be truthfully designated a spiritual "*Hippomolgian.*" Strife, discord and wrangling but poorly comport with the divine inculcations and habitudes.

It is said that a king, or chieftain, in South Africa was closely importuned by his christianized sons to be baptized; but he justified his heathenism by the existing divisions among the mission churches. "My sons," he said, "want me to be baptized. I say to them, Christians here, pointing to the Wesleyan Station, and Christians there, pointing to the Anglican monks. Christians there wont speak to Christians here. When one of them has converted the other it will be time enough to come to me." What a Upas tree is division! How disastrous are its effects, even on heathendom!

I would remark that—

2nd. *The prospective kingdom of Christ is hopeful.* As regards the unity, greatness and glory of Christ's Church, sometime hereafter there can exist no precarious contingencies. Surpassingly grand and peerlessly great it must become in the unseen, if not in the immediate, future. True it is, indeed, that the feuds and schisms, and divisions, and the unholy warfare by which it has heretofore and hitherto been beset, and by which it has been blotched, blighted and shrivelled, are calculated to cause the faith of the mightiest minds to stagger, and to cause the contemplation of weaker saints to reluctate. But mighty, great and united, the Church shall be, hereafter, nevertheless. Doubts and perplexities have environed and overwhelmed even some great men in all ages.

It is recorded, by a Greek writer of the life of Homer, that the immortal poet died of vexation, because of not being able to discover a riddle which was proposed to him by some fishermen at an island called Io. Hapless, though famous bard! A mendicant throughout life, and a suicide in death!

But before the auspicious and long-wished for day dawns upon Christendom, the Church universally must exercise more confidence and manifest more prayerfulness. Indeed, the Church may well blush because of her incredulity, apathy and torpidity, when compared with the votaries of heathendom. Homer scarcely ever makes his heroes to succeed, unless they have first offered a prayer to Heaven. He is perpetually, says Mr. Pope, in his excellent translation, acknowledging the hand of God in all events, and ascribing to that alone all the victories, triumphs rewards or punishments, of men. The grand moral laid down at the entrance of this poem, ... "'The will of God was fulfilled,' runs through his whole work, and is, with most remarkable care and conduct, put into the mouths of his greatest and wisest persons on every occasion."

When the Grecian chiefs cast lots, which of them should accept the challenge of Hector, the poet described the army as lifting up their eyes and hands to Heaven, and imploring the Gods that they would direct the lot to fall on one of their most distinguished heroes. As Pope translates it:

> "The people pray, with lifted eyes and hands,
> And vows like these ascend from all the bands.
> Grant thou Almighty, in whose hand is fate,
> A worthy champion for the Grecian State.
> This task, let Ajax, or Sydides, prove,
> Or he, the King of Kings, belov'd of Jove!"

How very like a fulfilment is this of the divine command, "pray without ceasing." Many professed Christians are not even good heathens. The writings of Livy and Cicero, of Balbus the Stoic, and the author of the "Life of Timoleon," reveal clearly how fully they believed in, and how strongly they relied upon, an agency which was altogether unseen and supernatural.

The first Scipio Africanus and Cyrus were paragons of piety, and would constitute superb models for imitation by Christian kings and heroes. Why, Xenophon tells us that when Cyrus led his army against the Assyrians, the words by which he inspirited his soldiers were, "*Jupiter, the defender and conductor.*" Was this not tantamount to the "Jehovah-nissi"—"the Lord of Hosts is with us, and the God of Jacob is our refuge," of the ancient Church? The motto inscribed on the banner of the heathen general was, however, not so exhilarating and assuring as that which the Captain of our Salvation has bequeathed to His armies—"*Lo, I am with you always, to the end of the world.*" Let me entreat every soldier of the cross to seize this promise promptly and to hold it with the utmost tenacity. And, by all the deep and great and boundless obligations which all Christians owe to the God-man, who once suffered for them; and by all the

the unspeakable and eternal blessings which hereafter they expect to receive from Him, I beseech them, both individually and collectively, to endeavour to have all his saints externally united, and to cultivate assiduously the spirit of "Christian reciprocity," so that every one may, when Christ next appears, receive His eternal benediction:—" Well done, good and faithful servant, enter thou into the joy of thy Lord."*

* See Appendix D.

CHAPTER X.

FACTS WHICH PRESUMPTIVELY PROVE THE UNITY OF CHRIST'S KINGDOM.

Christian union presumptively proved by facts—Robert Hall and Alexander Carson believed and practised it—Dr. Geo. Campbell says that axioms are not self-evident to all men!—One reason why Carson did not write on the subject, *i.e.*, its being self-evident—Christ my only Master and the Bible my only guide—Christian unity condemned neither by precept nor example—All sins are so condemned—This is a necessity—If universal Christian fellowship were a sin it should have been condemned even by anticipation—Paul apostrophized—It is like Paul's lost Epistle to the Corinthians—Quotation from history—Lectures on Baptist History by a famous American writer—The Rev. William R. Williams, D.D., of New York City.

IT was considered self-evident by good and great men, such as Hall and Carson, that all Christians are entitled to church fellowship. This presumption, I grant, may be met by a counter presumption. My opponents may say that open communion is presumptively false, as good and great men consider it unscriptural. Still, that which appeared self evidently true to the gigantic minds of Hall and Carson, deserves at least a deliberate examination. But it is dismissed by many of the other party as a settled question—as a thing self-evidently unfounded. What Dr. Campbell says respecting axioms not being self-evident to all minds is verified in this controversy. That which one party looks upon as self-evidently true, the other treats as self-evidently false. Surely extremes meet And we may well say, that none are so blind as those that will not see. The good Dr. Carson told me, that its plainness, or rather self-evidence, was one reason why he did not write on the subject. "If any man be ignorant," said Carson, using Paul's words, "let him be ignorant." 1 Cor. xiv. 38. When asked on another occasion, he replied,—" that which takes a man to Heaven ought to take him into any church on earth." What the Rev. Robert Hall believed, wrote and practised, the world know, and, therefore, I shall not comment thereon. Some say he failed in elucidating his doctrine and in justifying his practise; others say he succeeded. Let the Christian world judge. We know what Carson believed and what he practised, but we cannot refer to his arguments. Alas! we can not. Would that this subject had not been to him a self-evident truth, and that he had not been silent for other reasons; then we might not only have his profession and practise, but also his lucid arguments. Many, however, say that he believed and practised that which he could not prove. What! Carson believe and do that which he could not possibly show to be scriptural?

Writings of the mighty dead confront this allegation! Let any honest unprejudiced man read the writings of this profoundly learned and most critical divine, and afterwards say that he ever practised that which he did not believe, or that he could not prove that which he practised! Should he fail in such an engagement, few would have the hardihood to assert that it was not a solitary failure. But they were men—fallible men, so we base not our practice on their authority!

We call no man Master but Christ, and we take no guide but the Bible!

The Scriptures condemn Open Communion neither by precept nor example. All sins, if I mistake not, are so condemned. That all sins should be so is absolutely necessary; for where there is no law there is no sin; sin being the transgression of *some law*. In what minute detail were the sins of drunkenness, theft and lying condemned; and fornication was stamped as reprehensible by the King of Zion, both by precept and example. See 1 Cor. v. Even the venial sins, to use a Romish term, of speaking evil one of another, and of observing days and times do not escape notice—sins which did not unchristianize, or unchurch, while open communion,—the great, the enormous sin of open communion is no where condemned! Verily, this seems strange! But the strict brethren will easily solve the mystery by saying—" the thing did not exist—

there was no such sin in the Apostles' days." But it is useless to quibble; the difficulty still remains. Answer me two questions. Why did it not exist? Why was it not expressly forbidden lest it should exist, or why was it not condemned by anticipation? See 1 Tim. iv. When the Holy Ghost enumerates in 1 Cor. v., the things which disqualified a person for Christian fellowship, baptism is omitted. If the Spirit specified the things which were calculated to unfit professors for a place in the Church both at that time, and at every subsequent period of the Church's existence, why omit baptism, an ordinance which he knew would be both mistaken and neglected, if non-obedience unfitted for fellowship? But it is not in the catalogue. Remember it might, had the Spirit pleased, or thought it one of the indispensables! If any say that it would be superfluous because of the commission, so say I with regard to all others. If the duty of all to be baptized could be learned from the commission and the practice of Christ and His Apostles, so might the duty of avoiding idolatry, adultery, &c., be learned from the moral law. "If any man that *is called a brother*, be a fornicator, or covetous, or an idolator, or a railer, or a drunkard, or an extortioner; with no such a one not to eat." Why, Paul, did you not add another word, just one word—a word of only two syllables, the word *baptized*, and all would be settled? Was it forgetfulness or parsimoniousness! Why hast thou been so particular and minute in delineating the qualifications necessary for bishops and deacons in thy Epistles to Timothy, whilst thou hast neglected revealing that which the Close Communion Baptists consider an essential qualification for church fellowship? How much trouble, labour, and grief, would it have saved many of thy brethren in these latter ages throughout Christendom!

But, beloved Apostle, we charge thee with neither parsimony nor oversight, because thou wast merely the inspired amanuensis of the Holy Ghost.

In conclusion, I would merely say that this epistle was to guide, and, be it remembered, does guide other churches. And, respecting this omission, I would only say that which Dr. Carson once said to me respecting the Lost Epistle to the Corinthians—"it was not necessary, or it is contained in the other epistles."

I close this chapter with a quotation from the work of one of my most devoted friends, who is a distinguished scholar, a very great historian, and a consecrated minister of the church:—

"What safeguard, it may be asked, was there for true unity? Need there be any better, could there be any higher than the covenanted supervision of Him who walked with unwearied tread and unblenching eye amid the golden candlesticks, and who, to the end of the world, assured His loyal followers that this, His care, should not falter? The Godhead was pledged to the oneness and invariableness and all-sufficiency of the great source of their life and growth. There was, however, yet another wreath of perpetual union between the devout on the earth, and the great theme of their worship in the heavens. It was in the withdrawal of His own bodily and visible presence. In virtue of it the child of an imbruted Heathen in our days is made one in heart with the Psalmist of Hebrew lineage, and with the confessors of primitive Christianity, and with the German, the French, the British Christian whose ancestry and training were so divergent from his own. One Spirit stretches its unbroken accord over the wastes of the centuries; and the Church of the one God is one—radically, cordially, intrinsically, and inseparably one in Him, the Jehovah holding Christ the one Head, having all one Father, and keeping the unity of the Spirit in the bond of peace."—" Lectures on Baptist History," by Wm. R. Williams, D.D. Page 102.

CHAPTER XI.

CLOSE COMMUNION MISREPRESENTS THE HOLY GHOST.

The Holy Ghost is the Great Teacher—It would be incongruous and contrary to all reason and modes of procedure, were He to leave His people ignorant of that which is an essential qualification—It would be, that of which even selfish and fallible men would not be guilty—The late Rev. Alex. Campbell, of Virginia, was aware of this absurdity, and endeavoured to obviate it, by constituting the *Written Word* the sole teacher—Close Communion denies the truth of two things—The Bible is the Law Book of the Church, universally and in perpetuity—Were baptism a pre-requisite it would necessarily avow it—All sins and omissions are therein explicitly condemned—Were ignorance, or the neglect of baptism, a disqualifying sin, it would have been condemned by anticipation—The Rev. Mr. Laidlaw's testimony respecting the prospects of the Church at present.

IF the Spirit only can teach, then all who are taught are indebted to Him. Paul said, "By the grace of God, I am what I am." Then if the

Spirit teaches the believer his duty as to the Supper, and not have done so in respect to baptism, if the hypothesis of the Close Communionists be true, he does that which no teacher, however stolid, would have done. He teaches a man a duty which he owes to Christ and a privilege which, as the strict brethren say, were he in every sense entitled, he ought to enjoy, and leaves him ignorant of that which, according to their notions, would enable him both to obey the duty and to enjoy the privilege! Oh! Oh! Brethren, look at this!

The Rev. Alexander Campbell, of Virginia, the distinguished founder of the Disciples Church in America, and others, after his example, feeling the weight of this argument, or to obviate it, declare that the Written Word of itself is that by which we are taught. Let us avoid small beginnings of error.

Strict Communion denies one of two things:—First, it must deny that any are really Christ's sheep, or even His lambs, besides those baptized; or, secondly, if it admit that Christianity is not confined to so small a circle as the Baptist denomination, then, they deny the truth, or what is worse, they hinder the fulfilment of what our Lord said was the birth right of all His disciples, " They shall go in and out and find pasture." If the fleece they bear is sufficient to distinguish them from the goats, if not from the wolves, —if they know the Great Shepherd's voice and follow Him to the sheep-fold, if not to Jordan, who can debar them? Who dare deny them admission? Alas! that any should cause saints to be debarred access to the table of the Lord, and denied or extruded from the followship of the Church, for then the declaration—the blessèd promise made by our Lord to His sheep is nullified!—"I am the door, by Me, if any man enter in, he shall be saved, and shall go in and out, and find pasture."—John x. 9. Now, if it be granted that all the transgressions enumerated were not chargeable on the Corinthians, which I think must be admitted, then it is evident that the Spirit taught them how they were to act on future occasions with individuals who might be guilty of one or other of the crimes which disqualified. This was to be their law-book henceforth. When Paul would be taken away from them, and when all direct communications from Heaven would have ceased, this epistle was to be their guide. Who will deny this? Let us suppose a case which is supposable, but one which, for other reasons, is not possible. It is, that two individuals stood at the door of the Corinthian Church as candidates for fellowship; the one an immoral man, but a professed Christian, who had been baptized; the other, a moral man, a real, consistent Christian, but unbaptized. I ask, by what law could they exclude them? The rule of duty as to the immoral man was plain—"With such an one no not to eat."—1 Cor. v. 11. But by what law could the Corinthians exclude the other? If they seemed not to know their duty as to the expulsion of the incestuous man, how could it be possible for them to think, or know it to be their duty to exclude or repel an unbaptized Christian? If it be argued that they ought to know it from the law of Christ's commission; surely they ought rather to know, from the nature and obligations of the moral law, their duty as to the moral transgressor. If it be said that such a case as that supposed occurred not in Apostolic times, I grant that such a case did not occur, but I argue that as the Holy Ghost knew that it might occur, *and that it actually would occur*, made it more imperative to have it enumerated.

When commenting on SECTS SYSTEMS AND THE CHURCH, the Rev, Mr. Laidlaw says that, "*The Prospect is Brightening.*"

"It is most gratifying," he says, "to observe that we have come upon an era in the world's history in which sectarian jealousies are beginning to disappear. As the Church is awakening to a sense of her true mission, and is going out over the whole earth in search of perishing men, she is beginning to forget herself—her personal appearance, her carriage, her dress—and is coming to think mainly about how best to do her work. Representatives of all Churches who hold Christ as the Head, take counsel together concerning the translating and interpreting of Scripture and the building up the Kingdom of their common Master, and from Sabbath to Sabbath their children study the Word of God in concert. Christian Churches of every sect have begun to strive together in prayer to God for the conversion of the world. Ecclesiastical bodies are beginning to look only into the history and creeds of other ecclesiastical bodies not for the purpose of detecting heresy, nor for the sake of ascertaining more accurately the nature and magnitude of existing differences, with a view to a more rigid adjustment of boundary lines; but in the hope of discovering new features of resemblance and new traces of hereditary affinity, by which they shall be able to declare that they all belong to the same family; and in some instances the circle has grown so large under this process of investigation, that when the family re-union takes place, it must be held in one of the world's great centres, every nation under heaven being represented in the happy gathering. And throughout the mission-field and at home in the great city and the little village, different denominations are beginning to consider not how each community shall have every sect represented in it, but how they shall so divide the territory as to economize, both men and means, and still have Christ and His cause faithfully represented. Do we not hear in this the sound of a going in the tops of the mulberry trees, which shall soon prove itself the harbinger of a still better and brighter day?"—pp. 254-6.

CHAPTER XII.

FEARLESS INTEGRITY AN ESSENTIAL QUALIFICATION IN ACCOMPLISHING ALL REFORMATIONS.

Lord Byron's intrepidity—How, when a child, he corrected the Actor at the Theatre—Man's weakness and vaccillation shown by Jehovah's injunction to the Prophet Jeremiah—"*Diminish not a word*," even God's Servants have to contend against their evil propensities—Those who bear disagreeable messages are generally hated, as if they were the authors—The messengers of good news are received with favour—Moses was blamed by those whom he led through the Wilderness—God's denunciations are often very disagreeable, because He does not allow His servants to soften or conceal any part of His messages—Some ministers foolishly boast of their dexterity in avoiding the doctrines respecting God's *Sovereignty*—Commentaries written to endeavour to reconcile man's venial desires with God's Book—The Ordinances have been similarly treated—All Christains to be treated kindly but *faithfully*.

A STORY is related of the talented but unfortunate Lord Byron, when a lad, which characterizes his whole career throughout life. It is said that, when sitting as a child among the audience of the theatre at Edinburgh, he attempted to correct audibly an Actor, who was professing to mistake the moon for the sun on the stage by saying: "I tell you, sir, that it's the Moon and not the Sun." And it is well known, that Lord Byron, often suffered afterwards by telling people that their "*Moons were not Suns.*"

Perhaps there is nothing in God's Word which more clearly teaches the peccability of man, even of an inspired man, than the stringent and uncompromising obligations imposed by Jehovah on the Prophet Jeremiah,—"Diminish not a word," and through him on all religious teachers. Unquestionably the injunction implied the possibility of even an inspired Prophet being, through the desire for praise or gain, or the fear of martyrdom, unfaithful to his commission. Otherwise, why should a messenger of the all-wise Jehovah need such a caution? Shall a servant among men dread the consequences of tampering with the contents of a message to the friends or the enemies of his Master; and shall the servant of the King of Kings compromise his duty, through fear, affection, or interest? The caution supposes then the temptation, and experience proves that the servants of the Lord are under the strongest solicitations of an evil heart to be unfaithful in declaring without reserve the will of the Lord. When the truth delivered is of a disagreeable nature, it exposes the messenger to the same hatred, as if he himself was the author of the threatened calamity. The messenger of good news is received with favour; but the messenger of evil news is an object of horror. But the messengers of the Lord are not only exposed to the same displeasure with other messengers of evil, they are charged as malignant persons, who delight in the evils which they denounce as from the Lord. Men do not generally, in words, attack the Almighty, when they are displeased with his message, nor directly bring him to account for what is offensive; they bring the charge directly against those who deliver the message, or who urge them to consider it in all the relations of the children of Israel in the wilderness. They murmured against Moses, and instead of laying the blame of their calamities expressly on Jehovah, they brought them directly in charge against His servant Moses. In this way they gratify their resentment against the evil which they dread, or suffer, and hide from themselves their awful guilt in calumniating the Almighty. The things denounced by Jehovah were exceedingly disagreeable to the people of Judah. Though mercy was always held out to repentence, yet, as they were wedded to their idolatry and sins, they despised the Divine favour, or the way of a return to his service. They must have mercy as they desire it. When the absolute destitution of their temple and cities was presented, they were maddened with rage which they in reality indulged against God, and which was vented against those who carried His message. Jehovah at this juncture encourages His Prophet not to falter, and in the most authoritative tone, charges him to diminish not a word. Neither would God permit the threatening to be concealed, nor the language softened. The misconduct against which Jeremiah is here warned is often exemplified in every age, in delivering the message of God from the Scriptures. How many of the professed servants of the Lord tamper with His message to the children of men! How many of them conceal a part of the will of God, in order not to offend! Some openly avow their craft and glory in it as an instance of holy guile, which is supposed to be a great accomplishment in a pastor. Have we not often heard of ministers of Christ, who boast that they assiduously avoid the doctrines of Scripture that relate to the sovereignty of God, and the deep things of His councils? How extremely wicked is the presumption! They condemn the wisdom of God as folly, and profess to have found a way of dealing with man more likely to be useful. The truths of the Divine Word are not to be taken out of their proper places. By pressing them in a view in which they are not exhibited, in the Divine

Word itself, evil may be done. It is preposterous to think that any thing is revealed in Scripture which it is wise to conceal. It is proof of atheistical profanity.

God's will should, invariably, be delivered as revealed. "Diminish not a word." Is the Lord more jealous with respect to the message to be delivered by Jeremiah, than he is with respect to the truths of the New Testament? How strangely has the Gospel been moulded in order to suit it to the pride of man, and make it less offensive to his carnal mind! How strangely have the doctrines of faith, justification, &c., been modified in order to reconcile the Word of God and the wisdom of man! How many ponderous folios of commentary have been written in order to effect what will never be effected—a cordial union between the natural lusts of man and the statements of the Book of God. The many contortions of the language of Scripture may be traced to this source.

Many of those who are engaged in explaining the Bible employ their efforts in endeavouring to destroy the features of Divine wisdom, and make the Book of God a favourite with the world. The ordinances of God's house have met the same treatment. By the institutions of the great apostacy all the ordinances of the New Testament have either been laid, or modified by human wisdom.

There is not one portion of the Divine inspiration which has not been wrested. The Lord's people, when they have been allowed to return from Babylon have, in many instances, even thought it prudent to bend to circumstances, and by a holy guile, to persevere in those alterations and modifications which were introduced by the man of sin. How few churches dare take the New Testament in their hand and go through it, with this fearful caution before their eyes! Have not almost all of them, either added, or diminished, or modified? While we are bound to rejoice in all who hold the truth, and should receive them in all things in which we are agreed, we should not cease boldly and loudly, and constantly, to make this charge " tingle in the ears " of all our brethren, " *Diminish not a word.*"

NO SECTS IN HEAVEN.

Talking of sects till late one eve,
Of the various doctrines the saints believe,
That night I stood in a trembled dream,
By the side of a darkly flowing stream.

And a " Churchman " down to the river came ;
When I heard a strange voice call his name,
" Good father, stop : when you cross the tide,
You must leave your robes on the other side."

But the aged father did not mind,
And his long gown floated out behind,
As down to the stream his way he took,
His pale hands clasping a gilt-edged book.

" I'm bound for heaven, and when I'm there,
I shall want my book of Common Prayer ;
And though I put on a starry crown,
I should feel quite lost without my gown."

Then he fixed his eye on the shining track,
But his gown was heavy, and held him back,
And the poor old father tried in vain,
A single step in the flood to gain.

I saw him again on the other side,
But his silk gown floated upon the tide ;
And no one asked, in that blissful spot,
If he belonged to " the Church " or not.

Then down to the river a Quaker stray'd,
His dress of a sober hue was made ;
" My coat and hat must be all of grey,
I cannot go any other way."

Then he button'd his coat up to his chin,
And staidly, solemnly waded in,
And his broad-brimm'd hat he pull'd down tight
Over his forehead, so cold and white.

But a strong wind carried away his hat ;
A moment he silently sighed over that,
And then, as he gazed to the farther shore,
The coat slipp'd off, and was seen no more.

As he entered heaven his suit of grey
Went quietly sailing—away—away,
And none of the angels questioned him
About the width of his beaver's brim.

Next came Dr. Watts with a bundle of Psalms
Tied nicely up in his aged arms,

And Hymns as many, a very wise thing,
That the people in heaven, "all round," might sing,

But I thought that he heaved an anxious sigh,
As he saw the river ran broad and high,
And look'd rather surprised, as, one by one,
The Psalms and Hymns in the waves went down.

And after him, with his MSS.,
Came Wesley, the pattern of godliness,
But he cried, "Dear me, what shall I do?
The water has wet them through and through."

And there on the river, far and wide,
Away they went down the swift tide,
And the saint astonish'd passed through alone,
Without his manuscript, up to the throne.

Then gravely walking, two saints by name,
Down to the stream together came,
But as they stopp'd at the river's brink,
I saw one saint from the other shrink.
"*Sprinkled* or *plunged*, may I ask you, friend,
How have you attained to life's great end?"
"Thus, with a few drops on my brow.'
"But I have been dipp'd as you'll see me now."

"And I really think it will hardly do,
As I'm '*Close Communion*,' to *cross with you*;
You're bound, I know, to the realms of bliss,
But you must go *that* way, and I'll go *this*."

Then straightway plunging with all his might,
Away to the left—his friend to the right,
Apart they went from this world of sin,
But at last together they entered in.

And now as the river was rolling on,
A Presbyterian church went down;
Of women there seem'd a wondrous throng,
But the men I could see as they pass'd along.

And concerning the road, they could never agree,
The Old, or the New way, which it should be,
Nor ever a moment paused to think
That both would lead to the river's brink.

And a sound of murmuring, long and loud,
Came over from the moving crowd,
"You're in the Old way, and I'm in the New,
This is the false, and that is the true;"—
Or, "I'm in the Old way, and you're in the New,
This is the false, and that is the true."

But the brethren only seem'd to speak,
Modest the sisters walk'd, and meek,
And if ever one of them chanced to say
What troubles she met with on the way,
How she longed to pass to the other side,
Nor fear'd to cross over the swelling tide.

A voice arose from the brethren then :
" Let no one speak but the 'holy men ;'
For have ye not heard the words of Paul,
'O, let the women keep silence all ?'"
I have watched them long in my curious dream,
Till they stood by the borders of the stream,
Then, just as I thought, the two ways met,
But all the brethren were talking yet,
And would talk on till the heaving tide
Carried them over, side by side ;
Side by side, for the way was one,
The toilsome journey of life was done,
And Priest and Quaker, and all who died,
Came out alike on the other side.
No forms, no crosses, nor books had they,
No gowns of silk, nor suits of gray,
No creeds to guide them, nor MSS.,
For all had put on Christ's righteousness.

APPENDIX A.

THE LATE DR. CARSON AND HIS CHURCH AT TUBBERMORE.

"THE church at Tubbermore became Baptist by degrees. Some of the members were baptized before the Pastor. Owing probably, in part, to this circumstance, they have never regarded an obedience to this ordinance an indispensable condition of admission to the Lord's Supper. Indeed, they have carried the principle of open communion to the utmost extent, by receiving members into their body simply upon evidence of their conversion, with but little enquiry whether they agree with them on the subject of Baptism, expecting that whenever they became convinced of their duty to be immersed, they would attend to it. To the great majority of Baptists it will appear that this practice together with their open communion was not in accordance with the example of those primitive churches which, in other points, it was Mr. Carson's delight to imitate; and that its tendency must be to throw into the shade an ordinance prominent in the New Testament, and to dissever Baptism from the Gospel, of which it is so expressive an emblem. Certain it is, however, that Mr. Carson believed this plan to be consistent with the will of the Lord; and this fact, while it may seem to show that his views of Gospel order were not in all respects precise and clear, is at the same time a strong proof of his esteem, liberality and kindness of disposition. It ought, therefore, to bespeak for his writings a very favourable attention from those who are so loud in their complaints of the want of charity among Baptists. He was as charitable as their hearts could wish, and ever more ready to hold fellowship with those Pædo Baptists who otherwise taught a pure gospel than with such Baptists as he might conceive to have departed from genuine orthodoxy. Every Lord's day, for the last forty years, has this church commemorated the Lord's death by the breaking of bread, regarding it as binding upon them to do so, as often as the return of the hallowed time caused them to remember His resurrection. This is a universal practice among the Congregational and Baptist churches, both in Scotland and Ireland. As authority for it they appeal to Acts xx. and 7,—"And upon the first day of the week when the disciples came together to break bread, Paul preached unto them," &c., and from this they infer that one of the most prominent objects for which the churches met on that day was the breaking of bread. In their belief that such is a primitive custom they consider themselves sustained by what is known of the manner in which Christian institutions were observed for many years after the death of the Apostles. On this point they cite the testimony of Justin Martyr, who, in his second "Apology for Christianity," says:—" On the first day of the week all Christians in the cities and in the country are wont to assemble together, because it is the day of the Lord's resurrection. They then read the sacred writings, listened to an oration from the Bishop, joined together in prayer, partook of the

Lord's Supper, and closed by a collection for the widows and poor." This may be received as an interesting picture of an Apostolical order in its native simplicity before the rude hand of corruption had marred its fair proportions."

" The increasing frequency with the ordinance as observed among most Evangelical denominations is a pleasing feature of the present day; and we cannot but regard the extensive change from annual communion—a custom derived from the superstitions of Easter, to its monthly celebration as a cheering approach to primitive example."

Note by the Committee of the Baptist Publication Society of Philadelphia :—

" In admitting this account of the peculiarities of the Scotch and Irish brethren, the Committee wish not to be understood as favouring all the views and practices described, or as encouraging their propagation in this country. They believe that the mixed communion and the admission of unbaptised persons to church fellowship are in direct violation of scriptural authority; that public exhortation by laymen in Lord's Day assemblies is an irregularity tending to produce disorder and many other evils; and that Christ has given no express precept for the weekly observance of the Supper—but has simply required that as often as we do it, we should do it in remembrance of Him." Yet as the object of this memoir is not to defend particular points of doctrine, or order, but only to sketch the history of an eminent and beloved minister, it was deemed advisable to keep back none of the facts necessary to throw light on the circumstances in which he was placed, and the course which he pursued."

"Mr. Carson's church were accustomed to partake of the Supper in the public assembly during the morning service, believing that in this manner they made it an instrument of really showing forth the Lord's death, and proclaiming by visible emblem the great facts of the Gospel; and deeming the ordinance far more lively and impressive when thus administered in the midst of surrounding spectators than when observed, as is often the case, in general absence of the congregation."

"The solemn and painful circumstances of his death we shall lay before our readers by presenting them with the following extracts from a letter written by a gentleman who was studying with him, to Dr. Maclay, of New York:—

"DEAR SIR,—Your letter of the 5th of July last to the late Rev. Dr. Carson lies before me. As his hand is cold in death and his sons are greatly afflicted, it devolves on me to acknowledge your favour.

"Knowing that you and many others of our American brethren will be anxious to learn how he died, I shall endeavour to furnish you with a true, though brief account.

"He went to England in July to advocate the cause of the Baptist Missionary Society. For this purpose he travelled through many parts of England, and I believe most of Wales. When on his return, about the end of August, when waiting in Liverpool for the sailing of the Belfast steamer, it was nightfall, and in taking out his watch to ascertain the hour, he approached, unconsciously, to the edge of the dock, and was precipitated into the water where it was twenty-five feet deep. Providentially, there were persons near at the time, who, with the aid of a ladder, succeeded in rescuing him from a watery grave. His shoulder having been dislocated by the fall, he had it set, and was conveyed on board the steamer. During the passage he became dangerously ill; and though on his arrival at Belfast he had the aid of the physicians there, together with that of his son and son-in-law, Drs. Carson and Clarke, of Coleraine— it was all in vain, he had to go to his rest and to receive what he often termed the reward of grace. On Saturday morning, August the 24th, A. D. 1844, he departed in peace, aged 68. His remains were taken for interment to his residence at Tubbermore. Oh! what tears were shed! And what voices of lamentation were heard over the dear departed warrior! Never was there such an exhibition of sorrow in this country before. It would have pierced the soul of any one to behold the anguish of the old veterans who had stood by him for the last forty-five years. They looked for their captain, but he was gone! They sought their general, but he was no more! Having supplied his pulpit most of the time during his absence, it became my painful duty to do so on the first Lord's Day after his departure from our world. But such a house of weeping hearers I never saw before, and wish I never may again.

"You may be able, in some measure, to calculate the loss which the churches of Christ have sustained when I tell you what he intended to accomplish. After the death of his beloved and excellent wife, he told me that he never intended to take a holiday in this world. 'I will' said he, 'leave them all for heaven.' At another time he said, 'My head is full of books, I will write on till I empty it.' One of the first which he intended to give us was a treatise on the Atonement. Would that he had been spared to execute it! But God's purposes had to be fulfilled. The eyes of all the Presbyterians of this country, with a part of the Scotch Church, as well as many other denominations were waiting on him for some time expecting this work. At length he consented to satisfy their wishes. He had the subject thoroughly studied—the plan formed—authors read, notes taken, and the book itself all but written, when lo! he was not! for God took him. He intended also to write a book on the best mode of teaching the churches. He thought that ministers in general were lamentably deficient in this matter. When I think of all he intended to do, and which he only could do so well, I am almost overwhelmed with sorrow. You will be glad to hear that he left a good deal behind him yet unpublished. He had just completed a work on the characteristic style of Scripture, showing its purity, simplicity, and sublimiry, and contrasting the Bible and the God of the Bible with the gods of the heathen, as described by their poets.   *   *

"How irreparable is our loss! How successful has been his course! What labours has he undergone! What results has he achieved! What privations and sacrifices has he endured! How like was he to to the Apostles and primitive disciples! He preached the Gospel, through good report and evil report. Nothing could cool his zeal. Onward was his motto. When Christ was to be served, His laws obeyed, or His truth defended, no force of opposition could discourage or intimidate him. Many an Alps has he crossed. His arm was mighty when fighting the battles of the faith.

> ' He was a warrior in the Christian field,
> Who never saw a sword he could not wield.'

"What shall I say of his assiduity? For the past fifty years or more he was never known to idle one day. He laboured hard for knowledge. What shall I say of him as a scholar and a critic? Viewed in this light he was far above either praise or censure. The grand peculiarity of his mind was critical acumen. He always saw the bottom of every subject which he undertook to handle. The foundations of his reasonings were laid, either in self-evident truths, or in explicit statements from the Holy Scriptures. While his honesty of heart would not allow him to deviate a single iota from the truth, to accomplish any sectarian object. What shall I say of him as a Christian? Only this, that with all his classical, philological and philosophical acquirements, he had especially learned the humility of his lowly Master. With the collossal stature of a giant he possessed the meekness and simplicity of a child. May we all, in this respect, imitate his example. What shall I say of him as a theologian and minister? Nothing. Let his works and his church speak for him. Might I not safely challenge the world to produce such a church? In knowledge and understanding of the Scriptures, its members could teach many a minister. And is it possible that such a man can ever be forgotten? Never, till the last trumpet sounds! He, himself, once said of Luther, 'It requires an age to produce a great man in some departments.' But a Carson is not to be found in a millenary. Who is so blind as not to see that God made him expressly for His work? Had not the fire of God kindled his soul, would courage so romantic have led him to attack the hosts of the Man of Sin in their strongest intrenchments! His faith was bold as that of Jonathan when with his armour bearer he assailed the ranks of the Philistines. Of him may be said that which was once said of the celebrated Robert Hall, 'He is gone, and has left the world without one like him.'*

"Yours truly,

"GEORGE C. MOORE.

"Tubbermore, 27th September 1844."

---

* Extract from a brief memoir of Dr. Carson prefixed to one of his works by the Baptist Publication Society of Philadelphia.

APPENDIX B.

"THE LIFE OF REV. ALEX. CARSON, LL.D."

By Geo. C. Moore.

Giving an account of its Inception and Progress, in a Letter to his son, James L. C. Carson, Esq., M. D. and J. P., of Coleraine.

M Y DEAR DOCTOR,—

I presume it is now about thirty-four years since your father was called away from earth. And yet few, infinitesimally few, within the great empire, of which he was an ornament, have heard a jot, or an item, respecting him; except that which those who possess his writings may have gleaned from them. To the uninitiated this must seem anomalous. For whilst this illustrious scholar, peerless critic, and mighty theologian, remains mouldering in oblivion, many a man who was comparatively a mental and literary dwarf has had his name and fame blazoned by memoir and statue, not only throughout the British Empire, but the world.

In *America* it has been otherwise. For in that country, a few years after your father's decease, one of his former opponents seemed to gloat over the grave of his late controversial adversary, and endeavoured to avenge your father's critical inflictions by publishing garbled extracts from his works. This, to say the least, was ignominious. For thereby he endeavoured to entail upon your father's memory and writings a spirit of gall and wormwood. Your meek and gentle father's spirit, instead of his arguments, seemed the only vulnerable point at which could have been hurled a shaft.

Thence arose an apparent difficulty. Your father's assertions needed no vouchers, and his arguments needed no sustaining advocates. But the man, the minister and the great Christian polemic, required to be portrayed as a man of charity, blandness, and docility. For it has always, and in all lands, been thought impossible to cause a pen, when dipped in gall, to produce anything which is either salutary or odoriferous. Therefore, the question mooted, and after a short interval vociferated, from Halifax to New Orleans, and from Quebec to California, was:—"Who is to defend Carson? Who is there that knows enough of his private and domestic life that can prove that he exercised a kind and gentle, instead of a pertinacious and malignant spirit?" For the people of the United States at that time seemed to concur fully in the sentiment expressed by Sir Edward Bulwer Lytton, who has said:—"How are the difficulties of the task of the mental portrait-painter increased if the private history of the man whom he portrays is almost entirely unknown to him; if he has to draw every tint, not from the living face of nature and life, but as seen through the multiform and changing media of his published works? To produce a likeness of the man of which he can say, with unfaltering confidence, that it is true, is well nigh impossible. Because the sentiments of the lip and the pen may be very different from those which find embodiment in the actions and the life. In writing of our hero, we should always like to consult his valet."

It was not long after this important question,—" Who can defend Carson?" was asked, until an answer thereto, emanated from teachers in academies, from professors in colleges, from presidents of universities, and from a mighty host of Christian ministers, and also from one of your own sisters and her husband, Mrs. and Mr. Hanna, then residents of New York, unanimously nominating your obedient servant, because of my having been a student of your father, and for years an inmate of his family; and having been at that time the delegate of the Tubbermore Church to the United States.

Well, my dear sir, having been thus summoned to undertake that, which I then considered an Herculean task, was more overwhelming to me, than it was astonishing to many of my friends and adversaries. For a person, of my years and abilities, to essay writing the life of so very great a man, appeared to be preposterous. And having previously heard that the author of—"The Divine Legation," had dedicated one of his works "to the most impudent man alive," I feared, that my compliance, might justly entitle me to the unenviable honour. So, instead of vainly and joyfully accepting the high behest, I took time, both for contemplation and consultation. But contemplation and consultation, did naught, except to harass and embarrass me. The work to be done appeared to be fearfully onerous; but to refuse to try to perform it, I considered would, necessarily render me, both pusillanimous and odious. And with these impressions, without ignoring the duty, yet I endeavoured to shirk the responsibility by writing to your youngest brother, your father's successor in the ministry at Tubbermore, to undertake the task, promising to aid him in every possible way. Unfortunately, he declined peremptorily, either doing it himself, or aiding me in doing it. His refusal, however, instantly and absolutely terminated my hesitancy, agreeing as I then did with a great writer, that there are occasions when any even the slightest chance of doing good must be laid hold on, even by the most inconsiderable person. Therefore, because of my fealty to the GREAT HEAD OF THE CHURCH, together with my veneration for the memory of the dead, and my obligations to the living, who had invited me to perform the work, caused me to erect the best fabric which my scanty materials and my scanty abilities could have erected. And since then I have frequently thought that no man knows what he can do until after he has tried, and that the *temerity of youth* is often more productive than either the *timidity* or the *torpidity* of age.

In the United States the work has proved very successful, both for the author and the publisher, having passed through eight editions in less than eight years, and might since then have passed through twenty other editions, were it not for the bankruptcy of the publisher, whom it amply remunerated. And having caused *The Independent*, which is the great mouth-piece of the *Independent Churches* of America, and of the all but omnific *Beecher family* to declare when reviewing my book, that " The author has rendered a valuable service, not only to his late friend and preceptor, but also to the Church of Christ at large: and that henceforth and for evermore, no man will be able to charge the late Rev. Alex. Carson, LL. D., as having been a man of a bad spirit, &c., &c., I felt myself amply rewarded. Thus, the primary object for which the work had been written, was most satisfactorily accomplished.

Then, as regards the size of my book, I would say that, if it be small, it was made so designedly. Its brevity was predetermined; so when I referred to my scanty materials, it had reference to the *quality* and not the *quantity*. Brass, lead and clay, I have discarded, because compilers, collators, and diffusive writers can, in this age, find but very few readers. I think you will readily perceive how easily I could have produced two or three ponderous folios, when I tell you that the late Rev. Dr. Maclay, of New York, and the late James Buchanan, Esq., British Consul at that city, furnished me with as much material respecting your father, all ready for the press, as would form a large volume. Why, sir, the life of even the great Dr. Chalmers had to be abridged in America! So, whether right or wrong, my ideas on this point tally exactly with those published by the Rev. C. H. Spurgeon.

After having reached this country, from America, last year, some members of your father's family advised me to proceed to London in order to ferret out my stereotyped plates, and to see the justly renowned Spurgeon, with the expectation of having a new and enlarged edition of my book, and if considered advisable, all your father's works issued under the scrutiny and approbation of the great London preacher.

Well, after a long and very expensive search I found my plates, thanks to the honesty of Englishmen! safe in the vaults of a great London printer.

My reception by Mr. Spurgeon was very auspicious and fraternal. "Mr. Moore," he said, "I have had your book those twenty-five years past, and I like it very much." Then, in addition to this flattering announcement he promised to aid, by every lawful means, a new edition of my work, and of your father's works also.

This was no faint praise from the man who had proclaimed in a sermon preached only a short time previously, and published a few days afterwards (Aug. 2nd, 1877), in which he said: " We have no biographers now-a-days. There is no greater cheat than a modern biography: it is not the man at all, but what he might have been if he had not been something else, &c."

Under those favourable circumstances I would have proceeded immediately to have issued my work, together with some thirty-five original letters written by your father to the Rev. Spencer Murch, of Báth, England, who kindly sent them to me to form a supplement: only for an intimation which I received from the Rev. Robt. H. Carson, of Tubbermore, stating that you were about writing a life of your father. Well, Doctor, though surprised and somewhat disconcerted by this announcement, yet I was glad to hear that one of your superior powers was about to undertake to correct my mistakes, if there be any, to supply my deficiencies, and in fact to produce a work superior to mine, and altogether worthy of its great subject. Hereby, I trust you will perceive the exercise of my deference for you. But after having waited patiently over fourteen months, now the sad tidings have reached me from Ulster that because of your many pressing avocations, and of your very severe bodily afflictions, that you have been unable to perform the work.

I trust my work is performing some service to the best of causes, not only over North America but in the far-off lands of Norway and Sweden, where it has been translated and scattered widely those years past.   *   *   *   *   *   *

Now, in conclusion, I would say that as my health has been fully restored, and as my sisters and brothers are pressing me to return home to Canada, I wish to ask you as the great chieftain of your tribe, as the leader of the large, widely-known, and justly esteemed Carson family, what am I to do with those plates? Will your health enable you to write an elaborate introduction, embodying all your greatest thoughts and ideas respecting your father for my work? Or shall I proceed to London or some other British city, and dispose both of my copyright and plates to some publisher? Or, notwithstanding the fact that those plates contain portraits of your father and beloved mother, which, I think, deserve some place of conservation throughout all future ages, shall I be compelled to have them demolished and sell the type for a bagatelle?

It has been said, that "fraud deals in generalities." so I have ventured to detail as many particulars as will show that my labours as a biographer, and the burdens thereby entailed, have been, *neither few nor light*. Hoping to hear from you shortly, I remain, my dear Dr., your obliged friend and servant,

GEORGE C. MOORE.

Tullylinn, Co. Sligo, Ireland,
    Sept. 23rd, A.D. 1878.

APPENDIX C.

REV. DR. WILLS' LETTER.

NEW YORK, Dec. 13th, 1852.

DEAR BRO. MOORE,—
Your note came to hand two days since, and I take this early opportunity to reply.

As your note is mostly in the shape of questions, I had, perhaps, better supply what information I can to each, successively; though, first, I would say I am happy to learn of your welfare. Not having heard from you so long, or seen you, I scarcely knew what to think, as we are in such a changing world, whether you were alive, or dead, or what.

You inform me that seeing a letter in a newspaper respecting me, you were induced to write to know what I was doing in the city, and whether I had a church or not. You do not tell me the particulars of that letter; was it good or bad they had to say of me? As this is a world of so much evil, the Christian who seeks to follow the Lord, and oppose the Antichrist of all denominations in this day of widespread error, must not expect to have much good said of him. I am now out *antagonist to the Antichrist of the* Baptists, which the enclosed card will apprize you of, if you have not heard of it before. It would be too much to go into particulars in a letter. All I would here add is, that I have some opposition, and may expect more; but in the field no one drives me out, or my name is not Wills. My lectures were published as I delivered them, and I question if the Close Communion Baptists ever expected there would be such an exposure of their systems. When I have finished them I shall, please God, immediately form an open-communion church. The brother at Brooklyn you enquire for has not made any attempt as yet. He has been for six weeks at Flushing, but not preaching. He intends to join the church which I am about to form, and go out from that church, so that we shall have this city as a starting point, and intend, if life be spared, to form open-communion churches in any part of the country or States, where people are so disposed, and find the ministers if they wish it.

Your next question leads to both sorrowful and pleasurable feelings. You enquire for the health and welfare of dear Marian. Both surpass what we can describe or conceive. She left this world strong in faith and the comfort of the Holy Ghost, on the 26th of October. Three letters came to hand from her the same week she died. She had written one a month before, but by some means, which we cannot understand, we did not get it till more than six weeks after date, and two others written about a month after it, came to hand within two days of its delivery. In each of these letters she speaks of the comforting assurance she was receiving of her interest in Christ, and mentioned that she had experienced much blessing from my books. She mentions your name in her two last letters. In one she says, "Tell Mr. Moore, when you see him, for I know he was sincere in asking me if I loved the Lord Jesus, that I love Him because He first loved me, and He has drawn me with the cords of His love to Himself; He has led me into His banquetting house, and His banner over me was love." This was written Oct. 13th; on the 24th she died. In this letter, speaking of her health, she says: "What a mercy! after four months, without the least glimpse of getting any letter, I should now feel that I am nearly well, only that I am so very weak." But a letter from her uncle, accompanying this, told us that her case was hopeless. We, therefore, became convinced that the disease had been making rapid progress, and her sanguine feeling about being so much better did but indicate that she was in the last stages of consumption; but we thought, probably, that with the care and attention she was receiving, she might continue till the spring, before the disease accomplished its fatal mission. Mrs. Wills, therefore, began to arrange to go to England, but awaited another letter before starting, which letter brought the intelligence that she was up sitting by the fire, but evidently fast approaching her end. She arose from her chair to go and recline on the sofa, which, when she reached, she heaved a sigh, and was gone. What an unspeakable mercy, under such circumstances, to know that her faith to the last was strong in Jesus, and her soul greatly comforted by the Holy Spirit, The trial has been great indeed to my dear wife, and her health has also suffered much, but she is now somewhat better than she has been for some time. She desires her kind and Christian regards to you. Our little boy, Herbert, has been under the doctor's hands, but he is better, and we hope, please God, he will soon be restored to health. In other respects we are about as usual, and shall be happy to see you whenever you come to New York. Excuse haste. I have many letters to write to-day, and but little time to do them in. May the Lord bless you in all your undertakings, and keep you His devoted servant, is the prayer of your affectionate friend

S. WILLS.

APPENDIX D.

GOD'S WORD THE ONLY STANDARD OF APPEAL.

By Rev. Leonard Woods, D.D.

"IF a man wishes to ascertain whether he has a title to an estate, which has been left by a rich relative, he searches the law of the land respecting the inheritance. He examines the interpretations which have been given of those laws in the writings of the ablest jurists, and in the decisions of courts of justice. He diligently inquires into all the circumstances of the case, and into all the conditions with which it is necessary for him to comply in order to secure the possession of the estate. In this business he proceeds with great zeal, and without any delay. The interest which he has in the subject urges him on to complete his examination seasonably, so that if his title is clear, he may have the pleasure of anticipating the property, and in due time, of taking possession of it; and that he may guard against all mistakes and against the neglect of any measure which he ought to adopt. But what is the largest estate on earth compared with the heavenly inheritance? And what is the care and diligence which we ought to exercise in order to secure any earthly good, compared with that which we ought to exercise to make sure our title to the blessedness of Heaven? A little consideration will make it manifest, that the Word of God is the only safe rule. Neither the opinions of the world, nor the character of Christians, nor the particular experience of those around us, nor any views which we might be led to entertain of the nature of religion by our own reasoning, or by our own feelings, can be a safe standard. The prevailing opinions of the world, so far from being certainly right, are very likely to be wrong; because the world lieth in darkness. Even Christians are all very imperfect; and their faults may be more visible than their excellences; so that measuring ourselves by them would evidently expose us to mistakes. As to the religious experience of those around us—it may be true and saving, or it may be false and delusive. At best, it will doubtless be a mixed experience. And unless we have some higher rule of judgment, how shall we be able to separate the true from the false, the wheat from the chaff? If we judge ourselves from what we know of the experience of others, we shall be in danger of setting a high value upon that which constitutes the very essence of religion. Who is able to form a safe and perfect standard of judgment in regard to religious character, but that Being whose knowledge is infinite, and who is therefore liable to no mistake? Who but God perfectly knows the nature of the Kingdom of Heaven, or the necessary qualifications of those who shall be admitted into it? If any man should undertake by his own wisdom, without Divine teaching, to make out a description of the qualifications which the heirs of Heaven must have, he would undoubtedly fall into various errors, and his errors would misguide all those who looked to him as a standard. A rule of judgment, on which we can safely rely, must be formed by God Himself, or by those who enjoy His infallible guidance. If we faithfully attend to a rule formed in this way, we may expect that the conclusions which we adopt will be according to truth, and will stand forever. Believing, as all Christians do, that the Scripture is the only safe and infallible rule, we ought so to regard it in our own practice. When we go to our places of retirement to commune with our own hearts, and to examine ourselves; we have to do it with nothing as a rule of judgment, but the Word of God. Away, then, ye false imaginations, dreams, passionate excitements, mental convulsions. "To the law and to the testimony." This is our standard. And the right application of this to our own case requires the tranquillity and stillness which we enjoy in retirement. Here the all-important question arises: *Are we Christians?* We cannot safely trust to the opinions of our friends. They look only on the outward appearance. We go directly to our Statute Book, our sure guide. We open the Sacred Volume. We " ask for the *old paths*, where is the *good way?*" We turn to one and another passage of Holy Writ; particularly to the passages which I have quoted, and others of a like kind; for it is best to have particular places before our eyes, at one time this, and at another time that. Then looking to God for the guidance of his spirit, we inquire whether the traits of character thus presented to view, are ours. If we can stand the trial of God's Word, faithfully applied, we are heirs of eternal life. If not, we shall be cast away as dross. The Word of God, which we receive as our rule, is immutable. Other things change and pass away, but this *abideth forever.* The world, especially at the present day, is full of inventions. The active, restless mind of man is ever seeking after something new. But there is no such thing as a new religion, or a new way to Heaven. All that which deserves the name of religion, and which will be approved at the final Judgment, agrees with the same standard. In this standard there can be no alteration; and of course none in the religion which is conformed to it. All the true religion which will exist in our country, and in the world, the present year, and the present generation, whether commencing in revivals or not, and all which will exist to the millennium, will be just such religion as is described by our Saviour in His Sermon on the Mount, and just such as Paul describes, when he tells us what are the fruits of the Spirit, and such as is described in the various passages above cited, and in other passages of Scripture relative to the same subject. If we possess this religion, we are happy here and hereafter. If not, whatever our present appearances and hopes, we have no part or lot among the heirs of heaven.

APPENDIX E.

SECTARIANISM, A HUMAN DEVICE.

"IN the religious conflicts of the ages, the fiercest struggles have not been over the importance of obeying laws, which have been plainly revealed for man's practical guidance, but over human theories concerning secret things which belong to God, and which have been only incidentally referred to in Scripture, or even over things which have had no existence, save in the minds of those who have fought for them. And the feebler and more precarious a man's system of truth is, the more earnestly will he defend it. He strives to make up in zeal what he lacks in knowledge."

"But the framing of systems, and the dividing of

the world into religious sects, has had yet another, a more pleasing cause, man's sense of responsibility for the enjoyment of peculiar privileges. No good man has ever enjoyed any new heavenly experience without wishing that the vision could be made to tarry, that others might enjoy it along with him. Many of the great religious systems of the world, as well as many of the minor beliefs are simply tents erected over the peculiar religious experience of certain men. This is to some extent true of each of the great pagan religions, which has had its origin in a single individual. It is true in a happier sense of the various divisions of the Protestant Church, and especially of the Protestant Church as a whole. When Luther heard the words—"The just shall live by faith" sounded in his ears, he felt that God was speaking to him, and that the moment was one of solemn privilege, and in his heart of hearts, he wished that all could hear the truth as it had then broken in upon his soul. And finding those who afterwards became his companions in the Great Reformation work, he said to them, let us build a tabernacle for this truth, "The just shall live by faith," and accordingly the Protestant Church was established, and the one truth which has shone gloriously throughout it from the beginning, has been justification, not by works, or penances or prayers, but by faith in the finished work of the only begotton Son of God."

"It would be easy to show by numerous illustratrations, how different sects within the pale of the Protestant Church have arisen in a similar way. One man inspired by his view of one aspect of God's character has built a tabernacle in honour of the heavenly visitor, whose transfigured presence he has been privileged to behold, and the world has called the well-wrought structure, *Calvinism*. Another man taken up to the third heaven, in his contemplation of another aspect of the Divine nature has constructed a tabernacle in honour of the heavenly visitor, whose transfigured presence he has beheld and the world has called his skilfully contrived system, *Arminianism*. And so numerous have systems and sects now become, that there is scarcely a known feature in the character of God, or in the teaching of His word, which has not a separate tent erected over it, in which some delight to worship. While men hold firmly to their personal convictions, let them cease to regard their peculiar convictions, as so divinely inspired that they cannot be kept in abeyance, while they work together with others for the attainment of this common end, and diversity will be found a help, not a hindrance. Let a different course be pursued; let every man say of the system of every other—' I have no need of thee;' let each individual thus set to work, to build a tabernacle for his own opinion, as if it were the only opinion that had the inspiration of the Almighty within it, and even then let men have more regard for the structure of the tabernacle than for either the comfort of its occupant, or for any other purpose it is designed to serve, and it will be long before the church will be able to reproduce to the world that delightful kind of primitive religion, which found man walking with God, and worshiping Him everywhere, without the aid of any tabernacle."

"The Church of the living God is not a thing of rules and by-laws, and outward regulations. It is a spiritual house. The stones which compose it are lively stones, the redeemed from among men. It is not the fold that constitute the Church, it is the flock. And it matters comparatively little what the structure of the fold be, if only it is such as to provide for the proper shelter and nourishment of the sheep. If the sheep be adequately cared for, the walls of the fold may be of rough stones, gathered from nature's fields, or they may be of hewn stone, cut out of the mountain and polished after the similitude of a palace. And there may be many compartments in the fold; one constituted on one plan, another on another; or there may be many folds, and the architecture of no two of them precisely alike. It is the flock that is to be 'one,' not the fold."

THE BIBLE NOT SECTARIAN.

"The Bible is not a religious book in the sectarian sense. It is not an ecclesiastical book. It lays down no system of church government, departure from which shall be accounted heresy. It contains no elaborately formulated creed to which it asks the world to subscribe. It is the most liberal of all books. It is said that the testimony of history proves that the Bible is really a sectarian book, as may be seen from the great number of sects that come to it for authority. But the great number of sects that come to the Bible for support, or that profess to have their origin in its teachings, proves on the contrary that the Bible is not a sectarian book. Those sects have not their origin in the Bible, but in human nature. Sects and sectaries exist in all countries—countries in which the Bible is not, as well as countries in which it is; the testimony of history uniformly declares that in proportion as the plain teaching of the Bible is understood and accepted, sectarian jealousies and animosities disappear."

"To lift up the voice against wrongs that are done in the name of the Lord, is to forfeit the love of the nearest of kin, and encounter the hatred of all men."
—*Religion as it was and as it is,* by Rev. ROBERT J. LAIDLAW. Pages 250–4. Published by HUNTER, ROSE & CO., Toronto.

APPENDIX G.

THE RELATIVE POSITION OF ORDINANCES.

"The way in which the symbolical ordinances given by Christ for his disciples to observe are made relatively to bear, one upon the other, is an assumption of organized societies. These two symbolical ordinances we have considered. They have been exalted by the Church out of their place, and in the maintenance of this sinful magnitude of two simple institutions, the Church has been rent into a thousand pieces; they have been made to subserve the grossest heresies hell could invent, such as baptismal regeneration and the doctrine of transubstantiation. Under false notions on these two ordinances, every denomination of Christians has been racked, pained, and tossed upon the waves of bitter controversy. Every law of Heaven for the Christian Church has been constantly trampled under foot in the maddened excitement about these two ordinances, while comparatively no notice has been taken of the dishonour done to other institutions of Christ."

"We have not now to turn to the institutions themselves; the views entertained of them have been given under their respective heads. Our inquiry now is, how far they are relatively combined; what relation the one bears to the other; and how far there can be necessity to neglect the observance of the one until the other has been obeyed."

"It is maintained, by Baptists advocating restricted communion, that they are so connected, the one to to the other, and have such a relative dependence, the one upon the other, that it is ecclesiastically impossible to get at the one without first duly observing the other. These premises are decidedly false: they are so upon every ground that positive institutions of a different nature must, of necessity, be independent, one of the other, unless by an express law, they are united, as were circumcision and the passover."

"Turn to the law of the institutions from the great Lawgiver Himself—and there can not be the slightest inference that Christ ever intended that the one should have any relation to the other. As positive institutes of the Kingdom of Christ, they differ nothing from every other command of Christ, only that they are symbolical ordinances. They have a bearing, one upon the other, just as much as all the commands of Christ have, and no more."

"It is affirmed that Baptism has the first claim to attention as an initiatory ordinance to the Christian Church, and then the Lord's Supper, as a church ordinance, should afterwards be observed, and that this order ought not to be disturbed. Baptism, doubtless, has the first claim to the Christian's attention, but not upon the ground of its being the initiatory ordinance to the Church; the fallacy of this assumption has already been exploded. It is, therefore, enough here to say that this is not in the Word of God. It may be, for aught we know, in some of the heretical writings of some of the first apostates; but in the New Testament Christ added to the Church, and then they were baptized, as a profession of that faith which they had, the result of their being by His Spirit made members of Christ and heirs of the kingdom. But in point of time, when the ordinances were instituted, there is no ground for regarding Baptism as having priority of claim; it is unquestionably false to say that Baptism was instituted before the Lord's Supper, and we are compelled to conclude that there is not an individual who would assert it, were it not that they can find sufficient props to sustain their cherished dogmas and exclusive denominational creeds without dragging in John's baptism, and making it a Christian ordinance: but that sophistry we have exploded. The Eucharist or Lord's Supper was the first symbolical ordinance instituted: this was on the memorable eve of the crucifixion of Jesus. The ordinance of Christian Baptism was not instituted till after Christ's resurrection, nor observed until the day of Pentecost."

"It is affirmed that there is such a connection existing between the two ordinances, that none have a right to commemorate the Lord's death till they have been baptized. We ask for proof, for we have never found it in the Word of God, nor the shadow of semblance to defend the assertion; all the evidence adduced is to this effect (quotation from R. Fuller on 'Terms of Communion,' page 190). 'By the *standards of all churches*, baptism is required before any candidate is admitted to membership; and *this is the reason* why baptism has always been regarded as a prerequisite to the Supper.' Such is the 'proof' of a stickler for restricted communion among Baptists; surely he had better have gone to sleep than have written it! What does it amount to? Is it not, in effect, saying—'I have no Scriptural authority; but never mind, *hear the Church*—that will do when we can not get better evidence?'"

"We now turn to Scripture for proof that the position is a glaringly false one. The Supper was eaten before the institution of the ordinance of Baptism, and that, too, as administered by Christ to the assembled Apostles before He suffered, as Paul emphatically describes—'the same night in which He was betrayed.' And, after His resurrection, He was known to the two disciples at Emmaus as He brake bread and gave to them; and probably on other occasions, before His ascension, He administered the Supper to His disciples. They were unbaptized, for the ordinance of Baptism had not then been instituted. The words of Jesus in administering the Supper prove that nothing was required of the communicant but a discerning of the Lord's body and blood; and is it not possible that Jesus could have designed that the unbaptized should have been prohibited from commemorating His death, when He was the cause of such a striking example to the contrary, and enjoyed its reception, too, without any provision of the kind? Again: when He instituted

Baptism, He would, of course, have said that in future time Baptism must be observed by all disciples, or they must be prohibited from eating His Supper; but not a word to this effect proceeded from His lips. It is, in truth, just about as evident that one is depending upon the other, as that the salvation of man is depending upon either, which all will assuredly reject as a fatal error."

"We are advocates for Baptism, to occupy its right position, and for it to be administered in its true scriptural way to the legitimate subjects. We would be second to none in enjoining the observance of all things whatever the Lord hath commanded; but if any do not observe the obligation as we regard it in the Scriptures, but verily believe they have obeyed the command in another way, then God forbid that we should lord it over His heritage, and take rule and authority which he has never delegated. *What*, say to the people whom Christ redeemed with His own blood, 'you shall not come to commemorate His precious death, because you have not trodden in the steps that I approve!' Multitudes do this, and think they verily do God service, as much as did Saul of Tarsus when he persecuted the saints of God."

REV. DR. WILLS.

NOTE—The Author does not wish it understood that he identifies himself with Dr. Wills or others, who endeavour to prove that the first communicants had not previously submitted to Christian Baptism. I allow the restricted Baptists the full scope of all they claim, as to the priority of the appointment of that ordinance.

www.ingramcontent.com/pod-product-compliance
Lightning Source LLC
Chambersburg PA
CBHW030434190426
43202CB00036B/208